Return of the Hustle

About the Author

A natural-born entrepreneur, Eric Sheinkop has been challenging industry norms since the age of 16 when he set up his first music company, Bandit Productions. Initially running the business from his college dorm room, Bandit allowed Sheinkop to indulge his passion for indie music by developing emerging artists, securing major label deals, and negotiating lucrative TV commercial placements.

In 2008, after seeing the shifting tides that were shaking the foundations of the industry, Sheinkop co-founded Music Dealers, a global music licensing company that has paid out tens of millions of dollars to independent artists whose music has helped some of the world's leading Fortune 100 companies drive real business value through smart use of music in their marketing.

Since its launch, Music Dealers' proprietary technology platform has grown to become the largest global marketplace of emerging talent for over 600 TV networks, brands, ad agencies and video game studios. The Music Dealers catalog houses music from over 20,000 artists, living in 120 countries and is searchable by hundreds of meta-tags.

Sheinkop's thought leadership in using music to drive business results while also returning value to the music industry has made him a sought-after consultant and adviser for brands, film, and TV companies, as well as a frequent speaker at music industry, marketing, and technology conferences around the world.

Sheinkop has earned numerous accolades including recognition on Billboard's "30 under 30," Crain's "Tech 50," and the University of Wisconsin Madison's "Entrepreneurial Achievement Award." He was named "Music Man of the 21st Century" by Crain's Business.

As CEO of Music Dealers, Sheinkop broke new ground in music and brand partnerships, including brokering a deal with The Coca-Cola Company that secured Music Dealers as their global music partner and earned Coca-Cola a minority stake in the company. Such achievements led to Music Dealers being named to Inc. Magazine's "America's Fastest-Growing Privately Owned Companies" in 2015.

Sheinkop co-authored the acclaimed book, *Hit Brands: How Music Builds Value for the World's Smartest Brands*, published by Palgrave Macmillan in 2013. Landing in the top 10% of business books released by the publisher in 2014, *Hit Brands* is an essential guide to marketers on how to strategically and effectively use music to drive value for their business.

A native Chicagoan, Sheinkop is a passionate fisherman, skier, and frequent global traveler. Of note, Sheinkop was awarded the honor of running with the Olympic Torch for the Sochi Winter Olympics in 2012.

Return of the Hustle

The Art of Marketing with Music

Eric Sheinkop

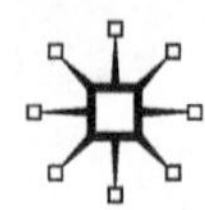

First published 2016 by
PALGRAVE MACMILLAN

Palgrave Macmillan in the UK is an imprint of Macmillan Publishers Limited, registered in England, company number 785998, of Houndmills, Basingstoke, Hampshire RG21 6XS.

Palgrave Macmillan in the US is a division of St Martin's Press LLC, 175 Fifth Avenue, New York, NY 10010.

Palgrave Macmillan is the global academic imprint of the above companies and has companies and representatives throughout the world.

Palgrave® and Macmillan® are registered trademarks in the United States, the United Kingdom, Europe and other countries.

ISBN 978–1–137–58200–3

This book is printed on paper suitable for recycling and made from fully managed and sustained forest sources. Logging, pulping and manufacturing processes are expected to conform to the environmental regulations of the country of origin.

A catalogue record for this book is available from the British Library.

Library of Congress Cataloging-in-Publication Data
Names: Sheinkop, Eric.
Title: Return of the hustle : the art of marketing with music / Eric Sheinkop.
Description: New York : Palgrave Macmillan, 2015. | Includes index.
Identifiers: LCCN 2015040561 | ISBN 9781137582003 (hardback)
Subjects: LCSH: Music in advertising. | Branding (Marketing)
Classification: LCC ML3790 .S516 2015 | DDC 659.1/045578—dc23 LC record available at http://lccn.loc.gov/2015040561

Typeset by MPS Limited, Chennai, India.

Contents

Acknowledgments

In advance, let me apologize for getting so emotional and long-winded. I have some wonderful people in my life and I usually don't take the time to let them know it.

First, I must thank my incredible editor, researcher, and project manager Zach Miller for always questioning and challenging me to prove my wild theories and making sense of all my chaos. There's no way I would have finished this book without you.

A very big thank you to Brandon Smith, Josh Burke, Tim Lincoln, Lyndsey Ager, Paul Sampson, Jessie LaBelle, and the incredible team at Music Dealers who put in the hard work over the past eight years to achieve impressive results. Without each and every one of you, Music Dealers would not be the success that it is today. It is because of you that I have the case studies featured in this book showcasing the great work that you do every day to help clients achieve tangible results through smart use of music. Your work has changed the future for thousands of artists around the world. Thank you for believing in the vision and taking it to the next level. We've been to war together and we'll always be family.

To all the artists from around the globe who I have worked with over the years and who have entrusted me with their precious art, thank you for letting me be a part of your journey. My days and nights are fueled by your music.

To our clients, thank you for giving me a chance. In the early days I begged many of you for one opportunity to prove the results you would see with an indie artist. Thank you for your belief and your role in changing lives by giving our artists a stage to share their music with the world.

To the people who book me to speak at conferences, the journalists who've helped tell our story and especially Stephen Partridge and Josephine Taylor at Palgrave Macmillan, thank you for giving me a platform to share my beliefs, vision, and passions.

Scott Lang, Ira Antelis, Emmanuel Seuge, Fredda Hurwitz, Scott McCune, you all believed enough in me to mentor me and be patient with me over the years to help me grow. I would not be where I am today without the opportunities you have given me and the hand-holding along the way. I am forever thankful for the time and knowledge you gifted me.

To my brother, partner and mentor, JJ, I'd still be in my room making beats if it wasn't for you. You have been by my side every step of the way, from sharing a room as kids, to helping create one of "America's Fastest Growing Privately Owned Companies." I can't thank you enough for all the guidance and unconventional teachings that have led to the amazing experiences we've shared.

To my Mom who set up my lemonade stand at age 6, and taught me how to hustle. Without knowing or trying, you taught me my most important lessons in business and life, especially how to respect the world and see the beauty in every situation. Anytime I talk about you everyone says, "Your Mom sounds really cool," that's because you are.

To my Dad, perhaps a bit tough at times … your support through every mistake, every passion, every situation – good or bad – gave me the strength I have today. You showed me by example how to live a life worth living and create your reality. As busy as you were, you were at every baseball game, judo match, and music recital. I have no idea how you managed, but it means the world to me.

My sister Joanna, being ten years older than me, you could easily have acted like you were too cool, but you took me everywhere with you and treated me like a friend rather than a little brother. Everything I know about talking to people and being in social situations I owe to you.

Ana, you were like another mother to me. Since birth you took me into your family, treated me with love and helped open my eyes to new experiences and cultures. Those experiences and our travels together have helped shape who I am. I am forever grateful to you for your generosity and care.

To the crew: Aaron Getsug, Miller, Stan, Rashaun, Altay, Marty, Tiago, Bri, Ben Lurie, it's an honor to have such epic homies. I've known you all over 20 years, and to this day I couldn't dream of better and more supportive friends.

No one has helped me grow more as a person and helped me focus on the important things in life than you, Judith. You are the smartest person I've ever known and make me better every day. It's overwhelming to think about how grateful I am for you.

Thank you all.

OK, now on to sex, drugs, rock & roll, and the art of marketing with music.

chapter 1

Introduction

Every generation in every society in every industry experiences revolution in one way or another, and the music and media industries are no different.

When you look at it on a global scale, revolution happens fairly frequently. You might then think their novelty would be lost, that their coming would be much less dramatic by now, that their impact would be more of a simmer than a boil. But that's not the case, thankfully. When revolution strikes, it hits like the first current of a river that's been long dammed. Some credit Napster's peer-to-peer file-sharing platform with the revolution that hit the music industry. Others say that the first crack in the dam emerged when the iconic Tower Records store on the Sunset Strip closed its doors in 2006. Still others say they first heard the grumblings of revolution when the sale of blank CDs for burning music outstripped the sale of music CDs by more than a two-to-one margin.

The music industry went through hell and back with the digitization of content

It is hard to say which one drop of water caused the dam to break. But through committing my life this industry, I can personally attest to this: The music industry went through hell and back with the digitization of content, and artists of all levels of popularity struggled to sustain their careers in an era of illegal piracy, unmonetizable downloads, and negligible streaming royalties.

As a result, artists have had to hustle more than ever before to grab consumers' attention among the flood of music that hit the market, forcing the whole music industry to look for new ways to commoditize their art. The bottom completely fell out from under what was previously considered a lucrative revenue stream.

Although devastation hit the music industry first, those same technologies that decimated the music industry don't exist in a vacuum. Today, the TV, Film, Video Game, and Brand industries are all fighting the same battle for attention and engagement. They too have to hustle more than ever to create real business impact.

A limitless choice of music, content, and media. This is the landscape of modern consumerism because of this digitization. Consumers have become more particular with the products they purchase, the brands they interact with, and the content they consume. They demand something of greater value beyond just the product and service of a brand. Brands of all industries – TV, film, advertising, and video games – need to find creative ways to provide consumers with that additional value lest they lose their business to a competitor that better understands the passions of their target demographic.

Music is the world's number one passion. It transcends language, gender, age, and geographic borders, making it one of the most powerful marketing tools for the Brand, TV, Film, and Video Game industries.

Music is the world's number one passion

In this book, *Return of the Hustle: The Art of Marketing with Music*, we explore this idea of using music to increase value to the consumer, demonstrating how the marketing power of music is helping drive better business results: selling more products, attracting more viewers, creating consumer advocates. Meanwhile, all of this is also helping empower the music industry to deliver value and return to the artists.

Many music supervisors have long understood this power, and many brand managers and creative advertisers have as well. But through the many interviews conducted for this book, what became clear is that successful music integration in marketing often happens more by chance than by design. Simply understanding the power of music to drive business is not enough. To be successful, you have to understand how to unlock that power to greatest effect.

By breaking down the elements from over twenty case studies developed from exclusive interviews with the industry's leading music supervisors, advertising creatives, and artists, and drawing from hands-on learnings with hundreds of our own experiences working with industry experts, we have identified within this book a formula that can be replicated time and again to drive optimal results. The same way a musician, regardless of genre or style, has a formula in the Verse, Chorus, and Bridge to guide them on creating a meaningful song, we have identified a formula for the successful integration of music in marketing. As with songwriting, this formula also has three parts – Attraction, Immersion, Extension – and can be applied as a universal strategy to ensure a meaningful music integration that delivers optimal business results to brands, TV shows, films, and video games.

It's my hope that by having a formula as a guide to achieve music marketing and supervision success, you will see more predictable business results and we can begin to better understand the tangible value of music in marketing, and that by doing so we can also deliver more value back to artists. Through understanding the real, direct results that emerge from effective use of music in marketing, we can demonstrate how this value cycle benefits brands, artists, and the music industry as a whole.

I've spent the last 15 years of my life integrating music into marketing initiatives. I've worked with over 500 clients to help them better connect with their consumers, thereby earning them more viewers and helping them sell more products. In the process, with my team at Music Dealers, we have helped thousands of artists – established and emerging – earning them tens of millions of dollars from their art. I see the potential that exists to deliver even greater value to all parties, but it's going to take a lot more hustle.

The music, media, and content industries need hustlers to push the envelope. If you're in these fields or aspiring to be, use these pages to hone your passion, to develop your skills, and afterwards you'll be better prepared to join a community of creative professionals who are all together helping resurrect the music industry.

The music, media, and content industries need hustlers to push the envelope

This is the return of the hustle.

chapter 2

The Marketing Power of Music

"Being a music supervisor is like being an A&R for a label, but the extra layer is telling a story with the music." – Tracy McKnight, Music Supervisor (McKnight, Music Supervisor, 2015)

A hustler, according to Merriam Webster, is an ambitious person who eagerly goes after what is desired ("Hustler," n.d.). According to dictionary.com, this is an enterprising person determined to succeed ("Hustler," n.d.). According to Urban Dictionary, this is someone who knows how to get money from others ("Hustler," n.d.).

According to us, hustlers are those who fight the uphill battle of bringing change to an outdated system in order to give the people what they want.

In the context of this book, hustlers are the artists who create music that redefines traditional genres and employ emerging technology like social media to blast it to the world. Hustlers are the music executives on platforms like television, film, video games, and commercial brands who are integrating music into their content in ways that were never possible before. Hustlers are the storytellers who understand that music is a global passion for consumers and are creating, promoting, and sharing stories with music as a driving force in their narrative. Hustlers are the consumers demanding more value from content, pushing the content creators to use music across mediums even more. Hustlers are the ones fighting the uphill battle of bringing change to the outdated music and content industries in order to give the people what they want – better experiences and more engaging conversations.

Historically, the music industry has been chock full of hustlers who championed each new era of music, pushing against the boundaries of what was considered acceptable in pursuit of the next great idea. However, when digitization fueled a saturation of music, the model of success – discovery, promotion, distribution – disintegrated. Piracy, file-sharing, and the ubiquitous internet equalized all music. Simultaneously, content evolved. Services such as Netflix and Hulu allowed consumers to choose *à la carte* which television shows to watch, opposed to subscribing through a cable package to a vast umbrella of shows and channels, the majority of which would probably go unseen. Films could be funded, released, and distributed online rather than pass through the former gatekeeping studios. Video games catapulted from an arcade novelty to a dominant form of entertainment for virtually every type of consumer. With the proliferation of screens – televisions, computers, tablets, phones – and the inundation of content by the TV, film, and games industries spread across them, brands and advertisers could no longer rely on traditional marketing to attract consumers.

Too much content was being created, at the expense of quality. The music and media industries needed innovators to guide them through this sudden shift – visionaries who understood the implications of this new multimedia landscape were sought to lead the charge rather than fight against the changing times. The industries needed a return of the hustle.

The Consumer Journey

Story, according to Merriam Webster, is an account of incidents or events ("Story," n.d.). According to dictionary.com, this is a narrative, either true or fictitious, in prose or verse, designed to interest, amuse or instruct the hearer or reader ("Story," n.d.). According to Urban Dictionary, this is a Cork, Ireland word for wassup ("Story," n.d.).

According to us, storytelling is the art of not simply conceiving the story, but also communicating that story in the most effective, most evocative ways possible through myriad mediums, from conversational dialogue to smartphone apps. Stories used to exist only between the pages of a book or in the airspace between an oral teller and the listener; now, with the global connectivity that technology and creativity have accelerated, storytellers have an array of mediums through which they can communicate with their audiences. Now, storytelling is changing the landscape of marketing.

For example, last weekend I was at a pop-up trip-hop party in a remodeled apartment on Chicago's west side to check out a glitch-grime DJ whose SoundCloud a friend had DM'd me on the preceding Friday.

I stood beside a precariously stacked column of speakers, watching my fellow trap lords Snap the technicolor stage, and I thought to myself, "The times they are a-changin'." No, literally. To the carnivorous delight of the surprisingly cultured crowd, the DJ remixed Bob Dylan's iconic "The Times They Are A-Changin'" with an overdub of drum and synth with violent, dramatic bass drops.

That moment – the Instagramming Millennials, the revolutionized oldie, even the DIY music-space – represented something much greater than just another ordinance violation and neighborhood nuisance. It is the new face of the media industry.

Consumers are virally sharing the stories of their real-life experiences. Content is repurposed and personalized to fit individual tastes. Places of engagement and interaction (whether that's online like social media or offline like the migratory Trap House of last weekend) are blossoming where consumers can cultivate their own experience without the intrusion of advertisements.

Currently, the media and content world is defined by communication. Through the proliferation of social media, brands of all kinds have been forced to evolve from traditional product-marketing practices to open and creative conversation with consumers. That conversation doesn't rely on annoying jingles and buy-one-get-one-free advertisements anymore. It's comprised of content that is authentic, that is story-based. Creators of all content types, whether they're brands, video games, television, or film, use story to guide consumers along the customer experience (CX) journey from awareness to advocacy.

The customer experience journey is the eight-step relationship between a brand and a consumer that takes place over multiple touchpoints. These eight steps are awareness, discovery, interest, interaction, purchase, use, cultivation, and advocacy. *Awareness* is generally knowing of a brand, though not fully understanding its products, services, or culture. *Discovery* is learning more details of the brand, which often happens through advertising or marketing initiatives. *Interest* is becoming intrigued with the brand, whether that's the brand's products and services or the culture and personality of the brand. *Interaction* is engaging with or researching on the brand. *Purchase* is the point of buying or subscribing to the product or service of the brand. *Use* is the using of the product or service. *Cultivation* is engaging with the brand after the product experience, such as through social media. *Advocacy* is being a fan of the brand, at which point consumers promote the brand by word-of-mouth referrals or even by creating user-generated content (UGC) for the brand, as often happens on brands' social media channels or even in some video games.

It's important to note how expansive the definition of "brands" has become. A brand is not simply the manufacturer of a product. Video games, television shows, films, and apps all qualify as brands, in the same way that Coca-Cola or Sharpie are brands. Despite the different consumer experiences across these varying industries, all travel through the same eight-step customer journey. The diversity of modern marketing, from TV commercials to onsite activations, has created innumerable touchpoints along that journey – the story of the brand fuels the evolution of the consumer experience through each step.

The more consumer passions that a brand can access in each step of the customer experience journey means it will result in a greater chance of converting passive consumers into brand advocates. Passion points are intrinsically valuable parts of the human experience – they bring value to consumers' lives in and of themselves. Because consumers face so much content every day of their lives, they have become choosier about which types of content they interact with; accordingly, they now have a higher expectation from brands and anticipate only the best quality of content in order to interact with it at all. In order to maintain the attention of their consumers, brands, video games, television shows, and films must create content that reflects their passion points.

In my previous book, *Hit Brands: How Music Builds Value for the World's Smartest Brands*, I define this theory as Social Empowerment. The outpouring of content has empowered consumers to become choosier with the brands they interact with – if they are not receiving something of value from the brand, they will simply change the channel. Swipe left. Close the browser. Social empowerment postulates that brands must reflect consumer passion points with every piece of content they produce in order to remain relevant in the marketplace.

Advertisers and media channels today must look to their consumers, truly understand what they are passionate about, and make an effort to enhance their experiences around those passions. While people are passionate about health, beauty, fashion, and sports, music is the top passion across the globe, and its value to consumers is still rising. In August 2015, music analytics company Next Big Sound announced that it had tracked over one trillion plays across Pandora, Rdio, Spotify, SoundCloud, Vevo, Vimeo, and YouTube since January of that year (*2015 Summer Industry Report*, n.d.). Music is a key companion to the life experiences of the modern consumer, as the innumerable "Workout," "Dinner," and even "Sleep" playlists on Spotify demonstrate.

No product, show, or even video game has been invited into people's lives more than music has. People score their lives with soundtracks, and brands are learning to do the same with the stories they tell. The media industry is getting more musical. Synchronization – when music is licensed for media like TV shows, films, advertisements, video games, and more – is on the rise, according to IFPI's "Digital Music Report 2015." Synchronization revenue, or "sync" for short, increased by 8.4% total in 2014 with huge gains in global markets: +46.6% in France, +35.5% in Japan, and +30.4% in Germany (IFPI, 2015). This increase is a reflection of a recognition of its importance by brands, television shows, films, and video games who are all investing more money in better music to tell better stories.

Music Strategy

Because music is one of several functions in a single piece of content, campaign, or overall brand, determining its Return on Investment (ROI) is one of the most difficult elements to measure, making it difficult to directly attach value to music in marketing. I recently worked on a McDonald's Olympic ad where the commercial had no audio other than the song. It became the most Shazamed commercial during the Olympics, went to number 3 most viral songs on Spotify, and went to number 6 on iTunes charts. Beyond that, brand product sales, specifically chicken McNuggets featured in the ad, increased 18% over a declining baseline during the airing of that commercial.

The band was ecstatic and as thankful as could be to my company Music Dealers and to McDonalds for placing them in the ad. The band knew without question that it was the commercial that made them an overnight, viral successes and the leading factor in them getting discovered and signed by a major label. However, the brand doesn't return the credit to the music for increasing its sales. Why? Because, it's just not common to attribute a real ROI on music use. It's not the brands' fault, it's just that there are no standards or common case studies to point to for these types of results. It's my hope in writing this book that the industry is able to start formalizing a process, one which produces repeatable, positive results and which demonstrates a true and measurable link between music integration in marketing and an increase in sales or a spike in content views.

Music strategy is the process of applying music to branded content and storytelling platforms that span the customer journey. There are three key functions to music strategy: attraction, immersion, and extension. Mostly, music strategy helps provide consumers with an intimate experience beyond the core products and services. Music attracts consumers, immerses them into the content, and extends the relationship between brand and consumer after or between product experiences. Broadly, in the context of the eight-step customer journey described above, attraction covers the awareness, discovery, and interest steps; immersion covers the interaction, purchase, and use steps; and extension covers the cultivation and advocacy steps. And this sequential consumer journey has been happening the same way for centuries.

Music strategy is the process of applying music to branded content and storytelling platforms

In fact, your favorite nursery rhymes were the original jingles, sung on the street to make people aware of new products and immerse them in an experience. Hot Cross Buns was a jingle to sell the ever-so-delicious, spiced English pastry associated with Good Friday. In the

1700s, vendors would sing on the streets to let people know they had the product, how much it was, and that everyone would love this treat as a gift.

> Hot cross buns!
> Hot cross buns!
> One a penny, two a penny,
> Hot cross buns!
>
> If you have no daughters,
> Give them to your sons.
> One a penny two a penny,
> Hot cross buns!

The first thing the music did as part of the marketing effort was attract consumers on the street. It got people's attention and told them pastries were for sale and they were two for a penny. That's a hell of a deal. The next thing the music did was immerse the consumer in the experience by extending the song beyond the facts, and made the song fun with suggestions of why you would need more than one hot cross bun. It allowed their imagination to wander about giving the buns to their daughters or sons or, potentially, other friends and family. The song connected the consumer to the product emotionally, way beyond what a written sign is capable of. And the third accomplishment of the music is the extension. Not only did people get that jingle stuck in their heads and walk away thinking about that song and thereby the product (the buns themselves), but the song started getting referenced in pop-culture, such as, in *Poor Robin's Almanac* for 1733, which noted: "Good Friday comes this month, the old woman runs, With one or two a penny hot cross buns."

Nearly three hundred years later, we're still singing that jingle. So when I say this is a new field, I don't mean it hasn't been done before. Music strategy has been applied time and time again, but it hasn't been formalized, standardized, or taught in a repeatable way – nor perhaps can it. As music supervisor Tracy McKnight aptly put it during our interview, music strategy and music supervision is an art. In the same way that the art of storytelling is part conceptualization of the story, part knowing how to communicate it, the art of music strategy and supervision is part creating or curating the music for the content, part knowing how to use it. The reason I've collected the top minds in the industry and analyzed their process is not so we can create a step-by-step guide to music supervision; rather, I hope to gather the music decisions of these experts into one universal formula that can be applied to any projects in any industry. That formula begins with music strategy functioning as attraction, immersion, and extension – just like the music strategy to Hot Cross Buns.

Music as attraction, broadly, is to make people aware of and interested in a product, service, or content like a show or video game. Attraction is probably the easiest step in this journey as people have their ears open and are always in need of discovering new music. If done well with consistency, this is the brand or network's chance to become a trusted source of new music for consumers. Achieving this would mean the brand or network starts to play a role in the consumer's life that goes far beyond the product or content. They become meaningful beyond their product and form a strong bond with the consumer. The good news is it's not that hard to do. Just pick awesome music.

I know it's easier said than done, but cool, unique music in a commercial is what will get people to turn their heads and look at the TV when they're doing dishes after dinner. Using the most popular song on TV, as the CMO's 14-year-old daughter requests, will not get noticed. People are so used to hearing the same song every time they get in and out of a car, that when it's used in a TV commercial, it doesn't even register. However, a cool, refreshing new song will not only grab ears, it will attract eyes to the screen. To do this with consistency will give a brand, show, film, or video game a musical voice and express a point-of-view on music, or what is referred to as Sonic Identity.

Much like you can turn on a radio station and know the type of music you'll be listening to, shows, commercials, video games, etc. all have the same ability to craft their music personality and point-of-view that consumers can come to expect and rely on. It's not simply a genre: it's the sonic identity of the brand.

In an eBook on the subject we released as a precursor to this book, *The Marketing Power of Music: Music + Television*, we compared the importance of creating a recognizable visual identity to the importance of a sonic identity.

Everyone agrees how important an image is to any brand. These include logos, colors, themes, and more. Creating a recognizable visual identity, and maintaining it across all touchpoints, results in strong recognition – for a TV show, video game, brand, or film. The same logic applies to sonic identity, which can be loosely defined as the music personality or sound of a show or brand. A strong sonic identity is important for the same reason that a strong visual identity is important: brand recognition (Sheinkop, *The Marketing Power of Music: Music + Television*, 2015).

When a TV show has a memorable sound, viewers engage in the first two steps of consumer advocacy: awareness and discovery. They begin to know the show through its use of music and sound, which helps distinguish it from the myriad other programs that are vying for their attention.

A show builds its sonic identity by applying its music strategy across its audio touchpoints: the various points where a brand, TV show, film, or game comes in contact with its consumer through sound or music. These points can include the title sequence, social media, live activations, the TV show, and anywhere that the show connects with consumers. The more consistent the music strategy, the stronger the sonic identity. The stronger the sonic identity, the more deeply viewers connect with the show.

Despite their similarities, there is one strong distinction between sonic identity and visual identity. Sound can do more than increase brand recognition between a show and its viewer. If managed with skill and creative foresight, sound can serve as an additional product in and of itself.

Consumers are choosier beings nowadays. They want more than to simply watch a TV show, just like they want more than to simply buy a product from a brand. They want their lives to be enriched beyond the lifespan of that original viewing, service, or product use. They want a relationship with the brands from which they buy, with the shows whose episodes they watch. They want something that they can take with them after the episode ends. If brands don't extend their relationship with consumers in that way, then those consumers can easily find another brand that will.

Music is one of the easiest and most engaging ways to do that. By building a strong sonic identity, a TV show, studio, or network can provide viewers with the greater customer experience that the modern consumer demands. A strong sonic identity with a consistent music strategy is one of the quickest ways to guide a consumer from awareness to advocacy.

When done right, people will tune into a show just to discover new music. They can count on a certain type of musical experience and they know they can trust it. Just like you go to certain restaurants because you know the experience will always be good and the quality will be consistent, viewers know they can always trust the shows with strong sonic identities to deliver quality music they can relate to. It's what gives them the ability to feel confident about sharing new music they discover from their shows.

This is Social Empowerment: focusing on your consumer's passions and enhancing those experiences to create a relationship beyond the product. In the case of TV, your show is the product, the viewer is the consumer, and, as music is the number one passion in the world, sonic identity is the way to create an enhanced experience for the viewer. When people tune into a show because of the music and with a desire to discover new music, the supervisor has enhanced the experience for the viewer by focusing on their passion.

Personally, I was never into vampire shows; however, I watched *True Blood* religiously each week because I knew I could always count on Gary Calamar, the show's music supervisor, to end the episode with a brand new song I knew I would love. This doesn't mean the songs are always the same genre; in fact, they rarely are. But they have consistency, just like professional buyers who work at stores fill shelves with different products, and the shopper knows that although there's different products, there is a brand consistency they can count on whether they're buying jeans, shirts, or jackets. There's something that ties the products together and makes shoppers feel comfortable and able to depend on a store for consistency. For stores to have this relationship, it's up to the store professional buyer; for TV shows to create this relationship with viewers, it's up to the music supervisor.

Having a strong sonic identity makes it easier to attract attention to new ads and shows, but it also makes the job of immersion easier. Immersion is perhaps the most important part of a consumer journey, because that is where the purchasing happens. In the video games, television shows, and film industries, music helps immerse consumers into the content; in brands, onsite music or product sound immerses consumers into the product/service. Many supervisors will humbly say, "Music functions to support the content." I believe that music functions to make consumers care about the content. Music is what makes it more than content. Music is what makes it part of your life.

Music is what makes it more than content

If you can make an ad, show, video game, or film meaningful in a person's life, you can bet they're not going to keep it to themselves. Nailing the right music and the right musical experience will ensure extension of your marketing. Once the marketing has attracted a consumer and made them aware, marketers need to immerse them in a meaningful and entertaining experience, and after their paid time expires and they no longer have the captive consumer, marketers need to extend the experience and make the consumer keep thinking about the product or content and even start to advocate for the product or content by telling their friends and talking about the product in a natural, organic way. I see supervisors as part of this marketing effort. They are in charge of realizing the marketing power of music by creating unique and exciting ways to attract, immerse, and extend, and thereby sell more products or capture more viewers.

Across all industries – television, film, video games, and brands – this definition applies; however, each industry has a different set of audio touchpoints through which they can apply music strategy. Audio touchpoints are the contact points between consumers and the brand that can involve music or sound, including everything from a commercial to a phone app. There are ten core audio touchpoints in each industry, some of which overlap and a few that are consistent throughout them all. These ten audio touchpoints are the places where music strategy can be leveraged in order to attract consumers to content or a brand, immerse them into the content or the character of the brand, and/or extend the relationship between the consumer and brand beyond product experience – this is the marketing power of music. Knowing when and how to manage music across these touchpoints is the art of music supervision.

The Music Supervisor

There are many notable publications on the subject of music supervision. It is not a new profession by any means, and has been at least vaguely a craft since silent films began to be scored by live piano music during their showing. However, too often the definition of music supervision differs from industry to industry, and even more often the duties of the music supervisor are undefined or reallocated to a less musically inclined coworker.

The Guild of Music Supervisors, a newly founded and important society, defines it thusly on its website:

> A qualified professional who oversees all music related aspects of film, television, advertising, video games and any other existing or emerging visual media platforms as required. In addition:
>
> 1. The Music Supervisor must possess a comprehensive knowledge of how music impacts the visual medium. The Music Supervisor works with the key decision makers and/or designated creative team to collectively determine the musical vision, tone and style that best suits the project.
> 2. The Music Supervisor provides professional quality service that combines creative, technical and management expertise with relevant proven experience. This specialized combination of diversified knowledge and unique skills is integrated into all stages of development, pre-production, production, post-production, delivery and strategic marketing of the project with regard to all music related elements.
>
> Music Supervisor Responsibilities include but are not limited to:
>
> 1. Identify, secure and supervise any and all music related talent, which includes composers, songwriters, recording artists, on-camera performers, musicians, orchestrators, arrangers, copyists, contractors, music producers, engineers, etc.: liaise and negotiate with talent representation, including legal, label, talent management, agency, business management, etc.
> 2. Liaise and effectively communicate with other related and involved professionals & support staff, i.e. directorial, production, editorial, sound (production & post), camera, choreography, studio & network executives, advertising agencies, clients, label executives, game designers, distributors and cross-promotional marketing partners.

3. Possess an accurate knowledge of all costs associated with delivery of music elements. Determine and advise on financial needs of project and generate realistic budget with respect to all music related costs. Deliver all required music elements within the established budgetary parameters.
4. Advise on feasibility of schedule based on release, broadcast, campaign or product delivery. Deliver all music elements consistent with specific technical requirements. Manage and/or secure legal rights of new and existing recordings, clearances of Synchronization and Master use licenses of pre-existing music, credits, cue sheets, etc. within scheduling parameters.
5. Determine the viability of, creation of and securing exposure or distribution of any music related ancillary product, i.e. soundtrack, single, video, internet downloads, etc. for the purpose of promotion or additional revenue streams. (*The Role*, n.d.)

We were lucky enough to speak with the Guild President, John Houlihan; the Guild Secretary, Jonathan McHugh; and the Guild Vice President, Tracy McKnight, among many other notable music supervisors across the four key industries on the evolving craft of music supervision. As Tracy aptly put it, "Being a music supervisor is like being an A&R for a label, but the extra layer is telling a story with the music."

Music supervision requires more than having an ear for good music; it's a craft based on the art of storytelling. Music and story are both powerful passion points in the hearts of the modern consumer, and both deliver intrinsic value that most products/services do not. But too often they are considered separate experiences. All stories – whether they're experienced in television, film, video games, or advertisements – employ music to support the experience, but only the most experienced of music supervisors know to maximize the intrinsic value of music as a passion point.

First and foremost, music should support the content, experience, and storyline. But by featuring audio – either by orchestral score, original soundtracks, or licensed music – of the same quality and intent as

recorded music, then storytellers are able to satisfy two passion points for consumers with one experience. So, to best support the story (as is the role of music and audio), storytellers must consider all audio experiences of the content in the context of music as an intrinsically valuable asset.

A key component of the modern music supervisor is this part of the Guild's definition: "This specialized combination of diversified knowledge and unique skills is integrated into all stages of development, pre-production, production, post-production, delivery and strategic marketing of the project with regard to all music related elements."

Music supervision happens throughout a branded experience – whether that's a television show or an ad campaign. To manage the music needs of all stages of development – from conception through to promotion – music supervisors walk the line between creative storytelling and prescient marketing. Music supervision is the craft of managing all music-related components of a storytelling platform, including television, film, video game, and brand industries, and is executed by applying music strategy in up to ten of the relevant audio touchpoints, in order to guide consumers along the customer journey and to support the story of the project.

As music is such a passion point for consumers, more comprehensive music supervision in projects results in a better customer experience; and a better customer experience yields greater returns for the brand, television show, film, or video game. Accordingly, many would call this evolved state of music supervision a win-win situation; however, I think it's more of a win-win-win situation. Because there's a third party benefitting as well.

The Music Industry

The marketing power of music in the television, film, video game, and brand industries is resurrecting the music industry.

The story of German audio engineer Karlheinz Brandenburg is well-known by most in the music industry. Among other accomplishments, Brandenburg is perhaps most remembered for his work in digital audio coding, which ultimately led to the foundation of modern audio compression schemes like the MPEG-1 Layer 3, more commonly known as the mp3 (Witt, 2015). A scientific milestone in that the audio file was compressed to a fraction of its original size without distortion, mp3 technology ultimately allowed consumers to download and share music for free. The CD era nearly disappeared, artists' projects were leaked across the internet before their official release dates, and consumers across the world turned to the internet as a way of acquiring all of the music they wanted and loved, even at the expense of those same artists whose careers were subsequently endangered.

Eventually, streaming services such as Spotify and Pandora emerged, providing consumers with nearly universal access to music that they craved and in a format that was safe from viruses; however, music sales continued to suffer. Streaming could not, does not, remunerate artists with an equitable amount of money to match the cultural value of their music. For example, in 2014 it was revealed that Sony/ATV publishers and Pharrell Williams were paid $2,700 for 43 million first-quarter Pandora streams of Pharrell's popular song, "Happy," in 2014 (Rucks, 2015). This means that for every 1 million streams, rights holders split about $60 of streaming royalties.

Despite the deplorable revenue from music streaming, it is perhaps the only barrier from returning the industry to the dark ages of the early 2000s in which music piracy dominated music consumption. Streaming services provide artists with a way to be discovered by new fans, as well as a way to track engagement and growth; however, until digital income for music matches the cultural value of the art, artists must find additional sources of revenue in order to continue their craft.

When Next Big Sound released its annual "State of the Industry" report in 2015, Music Dealers published an article that explored the

same conflict, entitled, "The Evolving Love Affair Between Brand, Artist, and Consumer."

"The shadow of crisis has passed, and the State of the Union is strong," declared the President during his State of the Union address.

The following night, I found myself hoping for a similar promise from Next Big Sound, an online music analytics platform that tracks artists' popularity, in its annual "State of the Industry" report for 2014.

"Brands. No longer a dirty word in the music industry," the report begins, echoing the principles that Music Dealers has touted since its founding. Artists are leveraging brands as partners to access their resources for widespread marketing, and to earn extra revenue to finance their craft.

And the feeling is mutual. Last year, brands took to working with artists more frequently in order to build long-lasting and meaningful relationships with their consumers.

According to a March 3 report by IEG Sponsorship, brands spent around $1.3 billion on music partnerships in 2014. More interestingly, according to Next Big Sound, brands are looking to work more with up-and-coming artists and not just "the Beyoncés and Lady Gagas of the world."

"Informed by data and with the right campaign," the report continues, "brands can provide additional leverage to spread the word, entice new fans that are otherwise out of reach, and actually help break an artist. In return, the kids think they're cool. Win; win."

People want to know what's hot before it's already popular. They want to be the trendsetters, the kick-starters, the go-to authority on what's-what.

As proof, monthly users of mobile music discovery app Shazam rose to 100 million in 2014 from 70 million in 2013, according to Shazam. Furthermore, the company recently announced that, after receiving $30 million in new investments, Shazam is now valued at roughly $1 billion. This all is based on users "shazaming" to identify new songs they're unfamiliar with. This shows people want new, undiscovered music.

So, yes – brands are smart for opting to collaborate more with emerging artists than big label stars, a trend that is rewarding those brands with greater consumer engagement and higher customer conversion.

"Interestingly enough, it is some of the lesser known, break-out artists that have led to the highest earned media value for [Target]," said Next Big Sound's report. "For instance, while Taylor Swift has 25x the number of followers on Facebook as Sam Smith, and 15x the audience overlap with Target, the brand saw $1.8 million in earned media value in the month following the Sam Smith release, compared to only $663,000 for the Swift release."

Target is well known for its exclusive music partnerships, in which the brand collaborates with artists to release albums or singles that are only available to Target customers. In 2013, the brand worked with 98 artists in exclusive partnerships and released over 200 bonus tracks, according to Target. Next Big Sound listed the brand's seven most profitable partnerships in 2014 and tracked the value generated in each campaign's first month. When totaled, those numbers totaled $6,885,000 in earned media value (EMV) for Target – and that's just from each campaign's first month!

Next Big Sound notes on several rising trends, including the continued digitization of the music industry, as demonstrated in the report's analysis of online music discovery:

> TOTAL PLAYS: 434,695,663,626
>
> +363% from 2012
>
> +95% from 2013
>
> Sources: Spotify, YouTube, Vevo, SoundCloud, Vimeo, Rdio
>
> TOTAL FANS: 17,335,824,480
>
> +202% from 2012
>
> +186% from 2013
>
> Sources: Facebook, Twitter, Instagram, SoundCloud, YouTube, Vine

Social Network Stats:

1. Fewer SoundCloud followers, but greater SoundCloud plays
2. Instagram is growing faster than Twitter as a platform for artists
3. About a quarter of all music-related follows on Twitter last year were for indie rockers.

The report's stats paint an interesting picture: people may be buying fewer albums, but they're certainly listening to more music than ever

> before. Additionally, 15% of artist-to-brand partnerships are with independent artists/independent labels. Though 85% are still working with major labels, brands are quickly noticing consumers' love of indie music, and will likely partner with independent artists even more into the years ahead.
>
> The relationship is clear: consumers want music, but aren't paying as much for it anymore; brands want more consumers, but can't build an audience on their own; and artists want to make music, but need a meaningful revenue stream to do so.
>
> But the state of the industry is not yet as strong as we all would like. Though music streaming is rising, revenue is dropping. Artists are losing their ability to grow in their craft, and the industry is accordingly suffering.
>
> But we're fighting to fix that. As this report clearly shows, [and from my own personal experience working with brands,] artist-to-brand partnerships can be the solution to these problems: for brands, consumers, and artists alike. As long as the interests of each party are upheld, these partnerships can provide consumers with meaningful content, brands with stronger engagement, and artists with significant revenue streams.
>
> The light of a strong industry is near, but it'll take some hustle to clear us of this shadow of crisis. (Miller, *The Evolving Love Affair Between Brand, Artist, and Consumer*, 2015)

Working with the television, film, video game, and brand industries is giving artists a platform for consumers to discover their music amid a saturated market, as well as concrete sales from upfront sync fees and performance royalties on the backend. What's in it for the artist? Money, fans, success.

With digital streaming, online video platforms, technological identification devices and even beacons, there is no question that there are more avenues for artists to be discovered and share their music with new fans. But how do they grab attention in the flooded sea of endless music, and where is the money? The majority of artists, especially new artists, aren't going to complain that Spotify takes away from their iTunes sales, because they're just trying to connect with new fans and be heard. Besides for the very top percent of ultra-famous artists, there are no loyal fans who are rushing to search for artists on iTunes these days. Artists are happy to just get on platforms like Spotify, SoundCloud, or even post their music to YouTube. But how do people find them, and, just as importantly, how do they get paid?

Watching people interact with Spotify for the first few times is something I find extremely entertaining. They're so excited to have access to endless music, but what do they do? Most begin by looking up and listening to their favorite albums and CDs they've had on shelves for years. They just go for what they know. They have no trusted music Sherpa to guide them to new bands, no old trusted DJ on Spotify or SoundCloud to lead them to new musical frontiers. Although we have access to more music, it's harder these days to know what we should listen to. We need a guide to give us something special, and we need it consistently so we always feel like we're cool and unique with our music tastes. After all, music is part of our identity. It's how we connect with people and feel part of a group. Our musical tastes make us special, but in the deluge of new music that assails the web every day, consumers need trusted curators of good, up-and-coming music.

consumers need trusted curators of good, up-and-coming music

Enter the music supervisor, the radio DJ for the modern age.

Radio DJs used to be – and still are, to some consumers – trusted to find the best new music and share it with their audience. Listeners relied on the DJ to filter through all of the music and, based on industry relationships, get the newest music first. If you were loyal to a DJ, it was because you felt a personal relationship with them. DJs fueled consumers' need to discover, to explore, and to share.

As selling ad space on the radio became more and more the driving factor that got music played, and after the exposure of the payola scandals, consumers lost trust in the radio DJ; however, they didn't lose their need to discover new songs and artists.

For the most part, radio no longer scratches that itch like it used to. There are, thankfully, a few specialty radio stations that still focus on breaking new artists and exposing new songs; for example, KCRW in LA, which is listened to around the world. These DJs scour the web, blogs, underground concerts, and indie trends to discover the music that is evocative, emotive, and powerful to the consumer experience. They hustle to find the songs that satisfy consumer passion points. They are also – surprise, surprise – the top music supervisors for the television, film, video game, and advertising industries.

They've undertaken the old art of sifting through and filtering all the 30 million+ songs and to find the special tracks that you want to hear, that you can feel comfortable recommending and sharing with your friends. These are DJs you can have a personal connection to and still count on nightly to deliver something meaningful into your life. So guess what they did with that talent? They took it from radio and brought it to TV.

The best music supervisors operate as DJs used to. They create strong relationships with artists so they can get the newest tracks released first; they spend their lives digging for special and unique cuts; they know the perfect build up and timing to expose a new artist and get them buzzing in pop culture.

The first step is creating the right vibe, and confirming a sonic identity, just like radio stations have. It's massively important to always stay 'on brand.' But the best music supervisors don't stop there. They then put the perfect musical lineup together so when they drop that new song, they've increased its chances of going viral and catching on. There's many tricks and tips on how to use this musical lineup to not only excite before and during the show, but also to keep the conversation moving after the credits roll. That's the end goal of the supervisor – use music to attract, immerse, and extend the relationship between brand and consumer.

In previous eras, artists would do anything to make a connection with a radio DJ. Now, they bend over backward to meet music supervisors.

There's plenty of conferences all over the world that celebrate the supervision craft and provide an opportunity to hear from the experts in person. The price tags for these events are in the hundreds and almost every event is filled. Students hoping to learn the supervision craft appear throughout the crowd, but the vast majority are artists trying to meet the supervisors and hustle their music into a show, ad, video game, or film. After the supervisor walks off stage, there's a queue an hour long of musicians waiting in line for their chance to pitch their music in hopes of getting it placed in media.

People say supervisors are the new DJ, but after seeing this adulation time and time again, I think they're the new rock stars. They're the untouchable, larger-than-life characters people will wait hours to shake hands with, and supervisors are the people who control and influence pop culture. But unlike traditional rock stars who cost you your allowance to see, supervisors are actually putting money back into the music industry and are considered a major source of income for artists.

These artists aren't waiting in line for autographs; they're waiting in line for potential checks.

Anytime a song is used in media, the supervisor negotiates with the artist or representative of the music on the sync fee – what the artist is paid by the project to use their music. The fee is most frequently based on three things: the type of media use, the time of use, and the territory of use. Types of media use include television commercials, online ads, video games, DVD home screen, TV show theme song, TV show background music, and at times even the characters of the show dancing to or singing it. All of these different factors affect the price paid for the song. Time of use is exactly as it suggests: how long will the media be live? This might be weeks, months, years, etc.; however, due to the longevity of online media, most supervisors try to license songs in perpetuity. Territory of use is the region in which the media will air, which can be local, regional, international, or all territory/global. Most internet licenses, and nearly all media that is repurposed to DVD or streaming services like Netflix, are global; however, online content can also be geo-locked to a specific region as long as the content creator has servers in the relevant regions through which they can moderate that content.

Understanding music rights and clearance is a core component of the role of music supervision.

When some of TV's original shows like *Star Trek*, *Cheers*, and *Grange Hill*, etc. were created, DVDs and the internet didn't exist, so the contracts did not explicitly permit the use of the original music on those platforms Now when a network wants to put those shows on DVD or video streaming sites, they don't have the ability to because of the music. It's amazing that the music contracts can hold the entire production up from having a new digital life, but it's a very real problem for Hollywood. Some of my favorite projects to work on and what many of these companies end up doing is stripping out all the original music and replacing it with new music, the rights of which they negotiate with the artists for "All media, in perpetuity, globally."

The last item to take into account when pricing is the popularity of the artist. The more famous, generally the more money their songs will cost. However, many supervisors, especially when it comes to video games, will try to create a Most Favored Nation (MFN) agreement, which means that all artists are getting the exact same fee and there is no negotiating the price tag. Many times in TV show supervision, the supervisors will sync independent artists or library tracks for the majority of songs placed in a production and save their budget for one or two famous tracks. Indie artists are very valuable to supervisors as they deliver the same quality sound as the big, famous artists at a fraction of the price. This is important to the industry because an average 30-minute TV show can have up to 20 songs placed in it, so the supervisors have to be very budget conscious.

This intense workload of clearing so many tracks in a production highlights the importance of a great supervisor. They must ensure that every song is servicing its core purpose of supporting the visual story, as well as acting as a key marketing tool, and that the licensing of songs is being done in ways to protect the production legally. Accordingly, the supervisor has to trust the artist or licensing company they're getting the music from. They have to know without question that the songwriter and publisher rights are legitimate and secure. Most independent artists will therefore work with a music licensing company like Music Dealers to help manage the conversation with music supervisors, negotiating splits of fees and royalties and cover insurance fees in order to secure a placement.

The top revenue-generating areas for artists are touring, selling merchandise, and licensing music to supervisors, in that order. But I'll argue that the priority of focus should be licensing first.

Why would someone pay to go to your show if they don't know who you are? They won't. Why would someone buy a shirt or hat with your band's name on it if they don't know who you are? They will not. So how do musicians get heard and discovered by new fans who will then pay to come to their shows and buy their merch? They have to land a sync.

The sync aspects of the music industry are the most sought after from all types of artists. Red-carpet famous or a basement producer, Hip-hop or Classical, local or international, sync is the most exciting area for musicians as it provides concrete revenue and a powerful platform to reach new fans. That is how the marketing power of music is resurrecting the industry, and all of the music supervisors, executives, and creatives interviewed in this book can testify to its success.

chapter 3

Brands

Converse spends millions of dollars building and running world-class recording studios and giving free studio time to indie artists around the globe. Red Bull has a top record label, Jeep throws free secret concerts, Taco Bell gives out free music by indie artists. The list goes on of brands that are providing experiences and content for their consumers that don't have anything to do with their core product. Brands are playing offense against the digitalization that's changed their world.

Why are they spending so much money on these areas that don't sell anything or integrate into their product offering? Something's up.

What's up is the amount of new brands and products flooding the market every day. Brands have a problem. There is more competition: it's easier than ever to create new products, manufacture, and market, and therefore new brands and products continue to flood the market daily. Luckily, brands can look to and learn from the mistakes of another big industry. The music industry was one of the first to really be hit by the digitalization of an industry. The music industry misjudged and played defense rather than offense. Now that we can look back and see inordinately falling sales for the past fifteen years, it's clear the music industry's strategy for dealing with digitalization was misguided and ineffective.

At one point, before digitalization of the music industry, an A&R from a label would have to discover a new talent playing live, set them up in a studio, hire engineers and producers, go through an expensive recording process, mix the album, master it, send it to get manufactured and pressed; afterwards, labels would then establish marketing channels and fight for shelf space in Tower Records and Blockbuster. That was the process when I was younger. But the students reading this book today are able to record and produce a song on their laptop with free software, upload it to iTunes and Spotify, and have their music in market the same day. That's why most of the students reading this book haven't once entered a Blockbuster or Tower Records store, and will never have the opportunity to do so again.

The problem that labels have today with new music flooding the market daily is that consumers don't care where the music comes from, as long as the product is good. Consumers have no loyalty to labels. They don't care if it comes from Sony, Warner, or a kid making music in his parent's basement, as long as the product is good. And today, everyone has the tools needed to create high quality music. What's happened in the music industry is the exact same thing that's taking place for brands today.

The same thing that happened in the music creation and marketing workflow is happening in the production, manufacturing, and advertising of products for brands. It's easier and cheaper than ever to produce and manufacture new products. Software has digitized the industry: brands no longer have to spend millions manufacturing products overseas. Brands can simply use nanotechnology to 3D print models and get actual consumer feedback or, better yet, they can raise money on a crowdfunding platform and earn sales without having to spend any money at all. With targeted digital marketing, it's easier than ever to reach consumers and sell products. So what's to make people care where the product comes from? What's to make people have loyalty to brands? As products flood the market, brands know they have to play offense and not simply sit back and wait to see what happens, which is what the labels did when they were faced with the digitalization challenge. They must create a connection with consumers that goes beyond the product. Brands must make consumers care.

Why should someone care if a shoe comes from Converse or if it comes from a few college kids designing them on laptops and having them manufactured locally? It's not about the product, it's about the relationship with the brand. This is Social Empowerment in effect. Social Empowerment requires that brands must create products and services of the highest quality, as well as craft a branded experience that delivers real value in the lives of consumers. Brands must show consumers that they understand them, they can relate to their pain points, and they can satisfy key consumer passion points.

Social Empowerment ushered music strategy into the brand industry. Music supervisors, brand executives, and advertising creatives craft storytelling messaging and experiential platforms that integrate music into the brand's identity and the consumer experience in order to satisfy that key passion point and deliver real value to the consumer. Music in the brand industry can be used in these ten core audio touchpoints:

Social Empowerment ushered music strategy into the brand industry

1. Commercials: Consumers are hit with over 2 million national commercial airings each month. License real songs by real artists to make your ad stand out above the rest (Our Platform, n.d.).
2. Artist Relationships: Brands and bands need each other: 68% of artist managers said brand partnerships were an increasingly important factor in adding value to an artist's career, which can yield millions of dollars in earned media for brands (We Are Frukt, n.d.).

3. Sonic Identity: Brands have always needed a consistent, memorable identity. Brands now turn to Music Agencies of Record to do that with sonic identity and build their music personae (Sheinkop, *How Music Agencies Are Shaping Sonic Identities*, 2014).
4. Product Sound: A product's sound contributes to its multisensory experience and sets it apart from competitors. From GE's appliance division to Estée Lauder's Clinique, product sound is being considered a "new branding frontier" (Byron, 2012).
5. Onsite Music: Whether your brand is a retailer or a restaurant, onsite music immerses the consumer into a branded experience. Shopping to music prompts the release of dopamine, delivers a sense of pleasure, and helps focus attention (Levitin, 2007).
6. CX Solution: 22% of marketers cited customer experience (CX) as their brand's single most exciting opportunity for 2015, but many struggle to create truly meaningful experiences. Music programs can guide consumers through the CX journey alongside the brand's products and services (Miller, *Can Music Save the Modern Marketer?*, 2015).
7. Social Media: Music is the third most popular conversation topic on Twitter, making it a hot discussion for brands to join and generate earned media that actually matters (Brandwatch, 2013).
8. Web Page: Having an online home for all things music keeps consumers engaged long after the checkout line. ABC uses its music site, http://abc.go.com/music-lounge, to give viewers news about the music on ABC programs, along with exclusive interviews and free downloads.
9. Live Event: Brands can use live events, festival activations, and sponsored tours to turn a simple concert into a multidimensional experience with unique, branded offerings: 51% of U.S. consumers and 76% of festivalgoers feel more favorable towards brands that sponsor a music tour or live show (Cardenas Marketing Network, n.d.).
10. Monetizable Assets: Owning the rights to the songs of their marketing campaigns means brands can even earn money from their

sales. Coca-Cola and other brands have entire assets divisions to monetize their owned music.

The following interviews and case studies illustrate how music was used to attract consumers to the brand, immerse them into the experience, and extend the relationship beyond the initial sell. When music strategy is leveraged across these ten touchpoints, brands become more than just product producers to consumers. They become curators of value – that's something all consumers will advocate.

Coca-Cola Case Study

Over 1.9 billion times a day someone around the world reaches for a Coca-Cola product. Coke is one of the first organizations called during a natural disaster in a foreign country. Their distribution channels are more robust and powerful than many global aid organizations, allowing them to deliver clean water to people in the farthest reaches of Earth in times of natural disasters when urgent need arises. That type of reach is mind-blowing, and something that took well over 100 years to establish. I am awed by the potential lifesaving impact this reach has, and after pondering on that, naturally my mind turns to thinking about the infinite opportunities that could result if you were to put that distribution and reach to work for music.

To be great at anything, we must have guides to help us along the way. Most times the people who make the biggest impact in your life are those that enter your world by chance rather than by design. In 2011, through my company Music Dealers, I formed a first-of-its-kind partnership with The Coca-Cola Company. Guided by Emmanuel Seuge, who at the time was Vice President, Global Alliances and Ventures at Coca-Cola, and now leads content creation for Coca-Cola North America, Music Dealers was brought in to help meet Coca-Cola's extensive need for great music to score their campaigns.

As our mentor on this journey into the world of big brands, Emmanuel taught us how to navigate the complexities of an organization the scale of Coca-Cola and deliver value to the company and their consumers in everything we do.

A key milestone in this journey was when Emmanuel made the decision to embed a Music Dealers employee in his team at Coca-Cola HQ in Atlanta as well as in the Coke offices in Mexico. From our position 'on the inside,' we were connected with people in over 35 Coca-Cola offices around the world to work on music initiatives in countries as diverse as Russia, Japan, Australia, and South Africa. The perspective gained from this incredible insight inspired and changed me, my company, and the many artists whose lives were transformed by the opportunities granted to us through Coca-Cola.

Beyond making introductions, Emmanuel set us up for success by identifying mentors across the organization to teach us how to work effectively in such a large, decentralized system. He connected us with a mentor in legal to understand the intricacies unique to big brand contracts. He paired us with the team who led the content creation process to show us how commercials evolved from a creative idea to a 30-second film reaching billions of people. He put us with PR experts to learn how to talk about the work we were accomplishing together. But arguably for us, the most important introduction he made was to Joe Belliotti, Director of Global Entertainment Marketing, whose task was to teach us how Coke thinks about and uses music.

We were like kids in a candy store running around the Coke building, trying to put music to work on every one of the over 3,000 products and 500 brands that Coke owns; however, we were lacking a deep understanding of why Coke uses music in their marketing. Looking back I feel sorry for Joe, who basically had to babysit me and rein me in to protect me from my own ambition. Joe took the time throughout the years to challenge me and my team to think about music in marketing from a more thoughtful perspective. I remember one example that really hit home. We were talking about the advertising that Coca-Cola created for their sponsorship of the World Cup. Joe taught me that while the primary purpose of the commercial is to celebrate and promote the partnership between Coca-Cola and the world's premier global soccer event, there are people who are not interested in soccer; so, the opportunity was to use the music in the commercial to get their attention and engagement in the campaign. He taught me that once you got their attention, you have to provide amazing experiences to immerse them in a way that keeps them fully engaged. Most importantly, Joe taught me that the number one way to get consumers caring about, and thereby sharing your brand's message, is to make the music meaningful and exciting enough that consumers want to share your content with their friends, thereby becoming advocates for your brand.

The lessons learned from working so closely with Coca-Cola helped Music Dealers expand our work to other brands, achieving global success and, most recently, inclusion in 2015, Inc. Magazine's prestigious "America's Fastest Growing Privately Owned Companies."

I've had the privilege of working alongside the people at the front lines of some of the world's biggest brands and learning from them the potential of what integrating music and indie artists into a brand like Coca-Cola can mean to increase brand sales and deliver significant money back into the music industry. It's no small feat, and the implications and responsibility would scare most music supervisors when learning about the delicate nuances of the job. But it's the implications of what's possible that gives me chills and keeps me and our team excited every day. With more expansive and wider reach than any label could ever dream of, the power to break new artists, share new music with consumers around the globe, and change music industry dynamics is very real. And who better to learn from about that opportunity than the person who leads that effort for one of the world's biggest brands: Joe Belliotti.

For a great number of Millennials, *Mad Men* did what their high school academic advisors could not – show them a career in which they could be paid to be creative. In the final scene of the final season of that wildly influential series, the creators gave a wink to another revolutionary milestone in advertising history: Coca-Cola's "Hilltop" commercial, featuring the now legendary tune, "I'd Like to Teach the World to Sing (In Perfect Harmony)" (The Coca-Cola Company, n.d.b.).

Talk about full-circle.

Commissioned by McCann-Erickson in 1971 and the most expensive commercial of its time, "Hilltop" portrayed a collection of multicultural teenagers singing what was originally titled, "Buy the World a Coke." Now referred to as one of the best-loved and most-influential ads in television history by marketing analysts and publications such as *Campaign*, "Hilltop" and its jingle became so popular that a group of studio singers – The Hillside Singers – were commissioned to rewrite the branded jingle into a recorded song. Entitled "I'd Like to Teach the World to Sing (In Perfect Harmony)" after the advertisement's tag, "I'd Like to Buy the World A Coke," The Hillside Singers' version reached #13 on the Billboard Hot 100 and #5 on Billboard's Easy Listening chart. Later, British-based pop group The New Seekers recorded a version that reached #1 on the UK national charts, #7 in the US national charts, and sold over a million copies in the UK. Rather than collect moneys on the backend, The Coca-Cola Company donated the first $80,000 in royalties to UNICEF under an agreement with the writers (The Coca-Cola Company, n.d.b.).

"I'd Like to Teach the World to Sing" represents a milestone in modern advertising for many reasons; chiefly, it signaled a slow transition into marketing driven by Social Empowerment and advertisements that delivered value to the consumer. Just as important, the campaign pushed brands to consider music as more than just background sound.

By partnering with the recording industry, for the first time in advertising history, Coca-Cola executed the three functions of music strategy – attraction, immersion, and extension – in one legendary song. Coca-Cola was able to embody the spirit of its brand, the idea of happiness and universal love, with a song for the first time, thus opening a way to attract consumers to the brand through music. The brand immersed viewers into the ad by filming a spot powered by music, thus pulling them in by accessing a key passion point, music. And finally, the brand extended the relationship with its consumers long after the spot aired by recording radio singles that people could buy and incorporate into their lives.

It's no wonder that Joe Belliotti, Director of Global Entertainment Marketing at The Coca-Cola Company, said that this campaign was arguably the start of music and brands coming together, the legacy of which he said he strives to maintain throughout the brand's campaigns by maximizing the marketing power of music (Belliotti, 2015).

Like many others whose career and passion are tied to marrying music and media, Joe's professional journey can hardly be considered conventional. After studying music production at Berkeley, Joe worked in the publishing arm of Maverick Records. From there, he worked on soundtracks and music supervision for films and TV shows through different studios such as Miramax and Warner Bros., until he eventually began getting calls about securing commercial songs and music celebrities for TV commercials and marketing campaigns. Later, he started a music marketing agency with notable music executive Chris Lighty, and consulted a key client of theirs, Coca-Cola, which he joined in 2010 to head the brand's Global Entertainment Marketing division.

"I think that if I look back on it," Joe said as he reflected on his path, "The evolution from the music industry, then using music to tell a story to picture, then using music to tell a brand story, it all sounds very thought out and logical, but it was not planned out at all. It just kind of happened that way because I liked the idea of pairing music with marketing, and really using music to help extend a story, whether it was the story of a scene in a TV show or telling the story of a brand campaign."

As expressed, the theory behind Social Empowerment can be applied to any consumer service, including marketing. According to the social empowerment model, marketing has to do more than advertise a product or service. Content is consumed at a higher rate than ever, and consumers demand value from each piece of content – including an advertisement – in order to even bother watching it.

Ergo, the rise of story-based marketing, in which brands use pieces of content such as advertisements as vehicles of story, a consumer passion point and thus intrinsically valuable. And just like in other vehicles of story, such as television, film, and video games, music is a key component in that story's experience.

"Whether you're trying to tell the story of what two characters are doing on-screen or if you're [...] trying to set the emotion [of the scene], you're really trying to do the same thing for a brand," said Joe. "You're really trying to set the tone and extend the brand into the audio space through the music you select or create."

"Coke has always had music as part of the way it tells its story. All the iconic Coke campaigns, like 'Always Coca-Cola' or 'Can't Beat the Real Thing,' have such a strong music layer," said Joe. "We've been involved in music since 1895. [...] The singer/musician named Hilda Clark was the first Coke ambassador [and was featured] in a print ad. In the 1920s, Coke was producing sheet music for people to sing around the piano. Then Coke started producing radio shows and even music itself in the '60s and '70s, most famously 'I'd Like To Teach The World To Sing.'"

A strong example of using music as a piece of storytelling is the use of "Wavin' Flag" by Somali-Canadian artist K'Naan in 2010 as

Coca-Cola's promotional anthem for the 2010 FIFA World Cup, hosted by South Africa.

"The tagline [for the 2010 FIFA World Cup campaign] was 'What's Your Celebration?' and it was [...] a celebration of the World Cup and Coca-Cola," said Joe. "And we found the song, 'Wavin'Flag.' The act of waving flags is so indicative of celebration, so it was really telling the story of our campaign through music."

K'Naan recorded a remix of the song, entitled "Wavin' Flag (Celebration Mix)," for the campaign and integrated the iconic Coca-Cola mnemonic into its mix. The song was played throughout the tournament, K'Naan performed the song at events for the FIFA World Cup Trophy Tour, and they even collaborated on twenty bilingual versions of "Wavin' Flag," each of which featured a different artist native to the localized market. For example, the English/Arabic version featured Nancy Ajram, a multi-platinum Lebanese singer and spokesperson for Coca-Cola Middle East, and was released in all Middle Eastern countries. All of this – as well as music videos and more events – continued after the final Golden Goal of the World Cup, in order to extend the consumer experience for as long as possible and retell the story in as many ways as possible (The Coca-Cola Company, 2013).

"How do you continue to use music to tell stories? How do you continue to use music to make that connection with consumers?" postulated Joe on the matter. "It's even more important today because media is so fragmented. Music, for me, is the one form of content that can live equally well in a digital space, on TV, on radio, in blogs, on social platforms like Twitter or Snapchat, [and on] products platforms – so music can expand and reach further than any other piece of communication."

Beneath the extension function of music strategy and a strategic touchpoint along the customer experience journey, live events guide branded experiences that are immeasurably more intimate, more engaging than any other medium. They embody the brand as an event, a hands-on experience in the real lives of consumers, and are critical parts of many brands' marketing strategies, including Coca-Cola.

"Coca-Cola live events [are] arguably one of the most important things that we do," said Joe. "Because our products are enjoyed in the physical world. Coca-Cola is a physical product, and that's where music and our product really come together. Not just the brand and what the brand stands for, but the product itself. Having a Coca-Cola when you're watching a concert or when you're listening to music adds to that experience, and that's where, from my perspective, you really start to see the power of the brand, the product, music, and our consumers coming together."

For the 2014 FIFA World Cup, hosted by Brazil, Coca-Cola began with a similar roadmap to its 2010 campaign: use music to bring the Brazilian experience of the Cup to the world, and bring the world's celebration back to Brazil.

In 2013, Coca-Cola worked with Brazilian singer Gaby Amarantos to craft the first version of the brand's anthem of the Cup, entitled "Todo Mundo" or "The World is Ours." A few months later, Coca-Cola worked with Brazilian-born singer David Correy and percussion ensemble Monobloco to produce its global FIFA World Cup anthem with English lyrics. From there, Coca-Cola partnered with Music Dealers to discover a lineup of emerging artists across the globe to record localized versions of "The World Is Ours" in order to spread the Brazilian experience to the rest of the world, and to likewise deliver global flavors back to Brazil.

"Then it started to feel global, because we were taking this music of Brazil, these amazing percussive rhythms and this idea of the World Cup, which was the campaign, and it started to express locally through local languages and artists putting their stamp on it," said

Joe. "Then, before the World Cup started, we took all those versions and we used a lot of them in Brazil. So it was like we were bringing the music of the world back to Brazil during the World Cup."

The cycle between the brand, the product, music, and consumers is a deeply integrated web of experience that began through the marriage of several consumer passion points. Music, sustenance, community, happiness – these all coalesce in the live events of Coca-Cola. The unfortunate part of live events, however, is that they are both finite and localized, which often limits the span of branded activations.

"That's the struggle, right?," said Joe on finding ways to maximize the content, music, and relationships a brand builds during live activations. "The way the brand works sometimes is either event-driven or seasonally-driven, so the campaigns are constantly evolving. […] But hopefully you find partnerships and artists in one campaign that you continue to extend."

"A lot of the artists that worked on the different versions around the world either have worked with Coke in the past or are now continuing to work with Coke," Joe continued. "We try to use the relationships that we build outside of the campaign for as long as they make sense."

Relationships between artists and brands are now integral to most emerging and established artists' careers. The digitalization of the industry saturated the market with music, making it harder for new artists to break through the noise. Both brands and artists quickly realized the discovery potential of music in marketing, as brands like Coca-Cola have the reach and influence that most up-and-coming artists could never otherwise access. For example, the shoe brand Converse launched its Rubber Tracks program, which provides emerging artists who can't afford studio time elsewhere a place to record at a high-quality studio facility.

"There are so many brands using music in so many different ways, and that in itself is a positive, because what it's doing is generating not just awareness through marketing," said Joe. "But it's also generating revenue for the music industry. The more that brands use music and the more they use it effectively, the more they will continue to use music, which is a great thing for the industry."

"The value that Coke can provide is in its marketing, its reach and connection with people," continued Joe. "The Coca-Cola Company has always been a great marketing company. The company has been marketing the same product for 129 years to generation after generation. With music we are always challenging ourselves to find more and more ways to for our marketing to benefit the brand as well as the music artists that are trying to connect to consumers. Coca-Cola is becoming an important part of the music ecosystem. I don't look at myself as a music marketer as trying to compete with the music industry at all, completely the opposite, really. I'm looking to complement what the creators and distributors are doing. When an artist looks to their tools on how they can break new artists – you've got radio, social/digital, PR, performances on TV. Having a brand's marketing efforts complementing that is something really that can benefit and add value to the music artist."

An example of Coca-Cola's push to support artists is its Coke Studio program, Joe explained. The original version of the Coke Studio franchise, Estudio Coca-Cola, first premiered on MTV Brasil in 2007 and featured live performances by local, emerging artists. Coke Studio Pakistan launched in 2008 as a one-hour television series that features live studio-recorded music performances by various Pakistani artists. The show provided a platform for emerging artists to perform to a national, sometimes global, audience and allowed both up-and-coming and mainstream artists a chance to collaborate in an otherwise impossibly intimate recording session.

The program saw such success that the franchise expanded into other neighboring regions, resulting in Coke Studio India, Coke Studio

Middle East, and Coke Studio Africa. International artists such as American rapper Nelly and Lebanese-British singer Mika participated in the series, sharing stages with local emerging artists Sherine Abdel Wahab and Karol Saqr, respectively. To further extend consumers' experience, each featured song is available for free download on the Coke Studio website immediately after the show airs (The Coca-Cola Company, n.d.a.).

"With those types of experiences, we're able to connect the world, [and] the artists will never forget that," said Joe on the Coke Studio program.

For the artists, those opportunities give them experiences that few could ever do in their normal lives. It's similarly true for consumers, who are given content opportunities that they could never otherwise experience. All of this is because of Coke and Coke Studios. With so much music and content flooding the market, consumers need a guide and a filter. Staying consistent with their sonic identity and music strategy, Coke has become that trusted guide of curated content for everyday music lovers.

One necessary step towards brands implementing more integrated music campaigns like those of Coca-Cola is defining key metrics of success, for both the brand and the artist, to justify greater partnerships and opportunities. Traditional key performance indicators (KPIs) such as brand awareness, music recall, and perception change are some important ways of measuring the efficacy of music in media; however, due to the relative infancy of the space, there remains a lot of room to grow.

"There's still a ton of opportunity," said Joe on the subject. "It really depends on how well we as marketers and the music industry as content creators can work together to define and create those successes. The more that we are able to capture and articulate how successful music is in a brand campaign, the more brands will be motivated to do it and the more artists will be motivated to do it."

"That said, you can always look at the typical types of research – where are people aware, do they recall the music from the campaign, did it help change their perception of the brand through all the typical sorts of measurements that you see? It's really about extending the reach of what we do as far and wide as possible. There are ways to measure that through impressions, expressions, and chart positions, [...] but I think there's a lot of work to be done on both sides to really nail how to capture the measurement of success for both sides. [...] Because the brand objectives are one thing and the music objectives are another thing, but the right campaign can drive both."

Moth & the Flame Artist Success Story

A prevalent theme of this book is the fact that the modern artist is not the same musician of the past, one whose pathway to fame and glory rests solely in the hands of A&R men and women at the major labels. And certainly not one whose be-all and end-all goal is to sign their song rights away for the marketing and distribution deals with one of those labels.

To say things have changed in the music industry would be beyond an understatement. Simply signing with a major never guaranteed fame and fortune; however, that dream is especially farfetched in today's time. The music industry is stabilizing and allowing labels to start reinvesting in artist discovery and development, however, artists today have to look to other sources to generate significant revenue and exposure for their work.

English artists Lucy Underhill and Jason Tarver understand this reality as well as anyone. Both have always pursued music as a career and their life's vocation. When the state of the industry darkened and the traditional model collapsed, they stuck with their ambitions and redefined their dreams in a world of new opportunity.

Like many artists, Jason and Lucy each began their individual music pursuits early in life. Jason first picked up the guitar around 12-years-old and played in bands throughout his teens and into his twenties. After high school, Jason said he juggled various "amusing" jobs in order to sustain himself as an artist and continue his craft.

"I think I was working in a pub and I thought to myself at one point, 'OK, if I could get a job of making music, anything, I'll be happy with that instead of doing this, because this is a horrendous job. I can't do this for the next 20 years,'" Jason said. "At which point I made a deal with myself. I said, 'OK, maybe you will be in a band at one point and you'll go on tour and everything will be fabulous and you'll never have to worry again. But in the meantime, you're going to have to find some other job doing music, because you have to get out of this'" (Tarver, 2015).

After forming this internal pact with himself, Jason said he returned to university to study music production and went straight into sound engineering in various studios afterwards. According to Jason, he continued to actively play in bands throughout his time as a sound engineer.

This new lifestyle led to a variety of "interesting" band projects, Jason said, because working in a studio invariably leads to meeting a ton of different bands. As a sound engineer, Jason worked with bands recording their EPs to songwriters producing tracks for licensing, and everything in between.

"I noticed when I was doing studio engineering work that the people with the nicer lifestyles were the people who were writing the music rather than the people who were playing it or engineering it," Jason said. "I remember doing a lot of very long hours, and the writer would show up, swing in halfway through a session, maybe add a little string section that they had been working on at home, and they'd take the files away."

"This was about the time money was leaking out of the regular music industry, so it seemed like a no-brainer to focus more on licensing at the time," said Jason. "For me personally, I sort of followed what was put in front of me at the time as a musician and as a writer."

Through his hybrid immersion in the music space, both working as a sound engineer and as an active artist, Jason became increasingly involved in writing for ad pitches, soundtracks, and TV. By being open to such collaboration, Jason and Lucy eventually teamed up to tackle both birds with one stone: sometimes writing and performing as a band, and sometimes writing as library musicians.

"It wasn't until about three or four years ago that I realized I wanted to make a bit of money out of music as well, because it's very hard to do so as a band," said Lucy. "The whole getting signed thing is tough to do. So I kind of wanted to do that alongside the other music that I do."

"We started doing stuff together that was mainly sort of library music and stuff for advertising, but then we found that we had lots of songs that didn't quite fit," Lucy said regarding the collaboration. "I've always played in bands, and a lot of my music is not really suitable for advertising. It's a lot darker and heavier. We didn't want to pitch them for a library, so we started this new thing that was Moth & The Flame. We thought we would see how it went and kind of do our own little band with that" (Underhill, 2015).

The music of Moth & The Flame is anything but conventional. Each experts in their own right in both authentic and commercial music, in writing songs to be performed on a stage and in writing songs to be synced to a screen, their work is defined by driving melodies and heartfelt lyrics, acoustic instruments, and organic sounds.

"I think it works quite well for advertising in TV, partly because I can't help but make things a little bit simpler because of the amount of

TV that I've been involved in," said Jason. "So, that sort of production theme comes relatively easily, I suppose."

Because of Jason and Lucy's extensive history in both avenues of songwriting, their process is often attributed to their blended experiences.

"Sometimes I try and write with complete free reins, because I think it's really nice to just not give yourself any boundaries and just do what you do," Lucy said regarding her process, which Jason described as being very organic.

According to Jason, some of his writing sessions are led by keywords, phrases, or themes that are commonly requested in the commercial word. At other times, he said, they've come out of those sessions with songs that "are never going to work in the commercial world."

"They were just born out of that environment, that cauldron of ideas," he said. "So I think it can go either way."

"[With Moth & The Flame], things come about in two different ways," Jason said. "We'll either sit down together, with a guitar or keyboards or whatever we've got at hand in the studio at the time, and we'll just start from scratch or throw ideas around to get a basic idea together. Or we'll start with an idea because maybe one of us had a chord sequence or a specific idea on an instrument to start a track with."

"In the studio, I'll sit there and I'll flesh out a basic guitar part and start building up the song a little bit, and while I'm doing that Lucy will sit on the sofa at the back of the room and scribble down lots of lyric ideas," Jason said. "And maybe two hours later she'll get the bare bones of something. So we'll look at those and go through the lyrics together. So, we'll get a rough thing together and then we'll leave it there. Then I'll come back and work on it, produce it up a little bit, and then we'll get together and do a vocal session. Or we'll do it remotely. Then we'll flesh out the production, I'll sort of mix it at some point, and then, 'Voilà,' we've got a track."

For artists like Moth & The Flame, creating music for their own projects and for licensing can be one and the same. Because of the need for extension, brands are licensing real music with increasing frequency and greater consideration, and the music in advertisements and the music in radio meld together. In fact, the song "Follow Me" by Moth & The Flame was originally written without a library in mind, Lucy said, even though it was eventually selected by travel accommodations company, Airbnb, to signify its brand relaunch.

"We definitely just wanted to write 'Follow Me' without thinking about anything in particular," said Lucy. "It was very much a song from the heart really, written like a songwriter would write without thinking about all the other stuff. I think that's partly why it worked actually, because it had that sentiment, that real sentiment, and then we could just sort of adapt it."

"I think if you write to a brief, it can be hard to keep that real sentiment in there," Lucy said.

When Airbnb began its brand relaunch, the company decided to integrate music into its rebranding strategy. Part of this process included finding an exclusive song that would embody the company's ethos of "belonging anywhere."

When Moth & The Flame received the brief for Airbnb's "Belong Anywhere" campaign, Lucy and Jason reportedly considered three songs they had already written that all seemed to fit. The original version of "Follow Me," Lucy said, was written about "the idea of going on adventures with somebody new and basing up in different places." This theme clearly already seemed aligned with the Airbnb "Belong Anywhere" brief, so they began adapting it to become more about travel and belonging in different places, Lucy said.

"[The adapting process] was quite mad," Lucy explained, "because I was in the middle of recording an album in Dorset, so I was kind of off in an entirely different creative place. But really it was just thinking about the lyrics and making it fit with what they wanted. They were really keen about getting some particular words in there, such as 'belonging' and 'home' and things like that. So, it just took a bit of juggling and sending things backwards and forwards between us and Music Dealers. I think we sent [Music Dealers] a few different versions and it was kind of an ongoing process to find the right thing."

Within two or three weeks of submitting the final version of "Follow Me" to Music Dealers, Moth & The Flame received word that Airbnb had selected it as the anthem for its rebrand and its "Belong Anywhere" ad campaign. The ad introduced its new symbol, the Bélo, "a symbol of belonging" and the symbol of the brand's new positioning in the market.

In a December 2014 blog on the Airbnb website, the brand stated, "When we rebranded Airbnb, our reason for doing so was much bigger than wanting a new, shiny look. We wanted to share with the world our story and the vision we have for our community and for the world. This message of 'Belong Anywhere' can feel like a pretty lofty ideal, and one that needs a little more to make it whole than, say, a new logo" (Airbnb, n.d.).

"To help share our message," the blog continues, "we chose the medium of song for all of the reasons mentioned above. We wanted it to be a story that could be universal and unifying for our global community. To do that, we partnered with Music Dealers, a group that represents the largest pool of emerging artists from around the world. Music Dealers understood us from the very beginning as our missions were well aligned: we wanted to work with an independent artist who could relate to our story, who perhaps even lives it, through music."

"Our artist community is very much rooted in the Airbnb community," said Josh Burke, VP, Strategy & Major Accounts at Music Dealers, in the blog. "A majority of these people are out there roughing it on tour. They aren't Beyoncé. They are driving across country overnight, doing different shows in different cities and countries looking to make connections and build their music, person to person. A lot of them use Airbnb to make this lifestyle possible. So the message behind 'Belong Anywhere' strikes to the heart of their meaning."

"What's beautiful about 'Follow Me,'" said Jonathan Mildenhall, CMO at Airbnb, in the blog, "is the way it describes a journey. It's not about searching for one destination of meaning and belonging. We are always evolving as people. We find different connections to different places and friends around the world at different times in our lives. Lucy has this voice and these words that break your heart and mend it all at once, and when we heard this song, it felt perfect. Universal, yet so unique to the Airbnb experience."

Focusing on the steps of attraction, immersion, and extension, after selecting the song for the ad, Airbnb and Music Dealers worked with Moth & The Flame to record a custom music video of "Follow Me" in an Airbnb listing in London. To heighten the launch further and increase attraction, the brand then flew Moth & The Flame to its headquarters in San Francisco to celebrate the launch of Airbnb's rebrand, where they performed a six-song set, which concluded with a live performance of "Follow Me."

"The nicest thing was when we landed and met everyone," said Lucy of the event, "and loads of the people from Airbnb already knew the words [to "Follow Me"]. That was great. With the live show, we didn't really know what was going on because it was so spontaneous just going out there, a sort of roller coaster in a way."

"It was really unusual to meet anyone from the company, and that was really nice to actually go there and have that contact," Lucy said. "I think often as a musician you're very separate, because often you're going through a music company and the publisher and probably an ad agency, so you never really have that direct contact.

I think we actually met the founders as well, so that was really quite special."

Uploaded to the brand's YouTube page, the music video for "Follow Me" is riddled with comments that demonstrate it was just the song the brand had hoped for: universal and unifying of its global community.

"J'aime bien, doux et réconfortant, jolie voix pour l'interpréter," said one comment in French. "Canzone simpatica e sicuramente adeguata allo spirito AIRBNB," said one comment in Italian. "Muito bom," said another in Portuguese. "Preciosa," said another in Spanish. "Loved it! Anyone know the chords?" said another in English, among many other comments that were equally as endearing, showing how one song can spread across the globe and communicate the same message across languages, cultures, and countries ("Follow Me," n.d.).

For any company that undergoes a brand relaunch, the goal is to onboard new customers to the eight-step CX consumer journey, and to guide them along it for as many steps as possible. In order to do so, the brand must create something of genuine value that consumers will discover, enjoy, and hopefully share. Those are the same steps as music strategy: attraction, immersion, and extension. By going the extra step to work with a real band and create a music video, Airbnb accomplished exactly that. "Follow Me" was a song that not only fit the brand, it also defined its new sonic identity. As a real song, created with the same care that any other artist would write a song for an album, "Follow Me" was music that people would want to listen to, and not just something catchy that they can't get out of their head.

This is what attracted so many people to the brand during its relaunch and, for many, began the eight-step consumer journey by introducing them to Airbnb and providing them with an interesting piece of content. For some, this helped immerse them into the brand and even interact with Airbnb enough to join its community and list their homes. Furthermore, for others it also encouraged them to extend the relationship with the brand into cultivation as they sought more content, such as the blog explaining the brand's sonic identity, and into advocacy as they shared the video with friends.

Commissioning the production of a brand anthem like Airbnb's "Follow Me" is not at all a breakthrough in the industry. Since the first dalliance between music and branding in the formative years of advertising, custom songs have often been a tool to establish brand recognition. Contemporarily, many brands leverage music in this way. Airbnb's particular use of music in its relaunch, however, signifies an industry shift towards authentic music like Moth & The Flame's "Follow Me," and away from kitsch jingles of yesteryear.

"I think what people ask for a lot these days more than a few years ago is more for a song rather than a piece of music," said Jason on this evolution. "I hate the word, but a 'jingle.' That's not a word you hear much anymore. People generally want a song, and that was very much the experience with Airbnb. You want a piece of music that has more value than perhaps an instrumental that took some guy in a studio an afternoon to knock up. I think people want more of an emotional investment in a song. You get that in a song rather than in a piece of music. Once something becomes a song, with a theme, with a vocal, it has something more behind it. It has three dimensions rather than two."

The difference between simple pieces of music and real songs is a subtle distinction, one which is more easily felt than defined. Pieces of music, or 'jingles' as Jason put it, are written in order to fulfill a brief rather than to engage and immerse a fan, and rarely have the same heart as a song that was composed with the express intention of emotionally connecting with its audience.

Once again, it's a subtle distinction, but many people can feel the difference between authentic music and stock tracks.

"I think [the shift in people wanting a song rather than a stock track] happened around 2009 or 2010," said Jason. "There was a definite shift, certainly in the UK. You started seeing a lot more top-lines appearing on adverts. [...] From an authentication point of view, having a top-line and vocals brought more kudos to a piece with music, whereas in the past you could get away with using instrumentals for an advert or for a TV sync or spot."

"People were asking for more [from the music in commercial media], and I think that's how the trend has come about," said Jason.

Many music supervisors have agreed with Jason and Lucy, stating that the power of authentic music can be a strong pull for consumers to connect with an ad and afterwards engage with the brand. These moments of genuineness are the strongest milestones along the consumer journey from passive customer to brand advocate.

That priceless value of a strong partnership with a real artist perfectly explains the motivation behind Airbnb's collaboration with Moth & The Flame.

"[Creating videos and hosting a live concert makes] it seem like they really have authenticity, and to show it as a real band and not just someone writing to order or it's not just music that they've bought from a library. It's a real thing," Lucy said. "When I watch TV, I can tell when music's got a bit more integrity to it. I think it can make a big difference by being a real artist."

Though Moth & The Flame is, according to Lucy's site, birdnoise.net, a "singer/songwriter-led music production team providing bespoke music to the advertising industry, production music companies and recording artists," they do access the heartfelt core of music by focusing first and foremost on creating music that is powerful and touching (Birdnoise, n.d.).

"Our niche is creating music that is a little more handmade, leftfield and indie in its approach," the site reads. "As multi-instrumentalists we use live instruments as much as we can, depending on the brief. We're also adept at creating work inspired by current trends in popular, rock and indie music."

"Our core aim is to create music that is honest, authentic and to always put a little heart & soul into it," the site continues.

On the band's main site, mothandtheflame.co.uk, seven honest and authentic tracks are available to preview, including a version of "Follow Me." Primarily based in the Dorset countryside of England, one can feel and appreciate the true fusion of indie-pop with the area's idyllic landscape. In fact, their bespoke music has been recognized for its genuine sound. In October 2014, they were awarded Best Folk Track for the song "All the Pieces" at the Library Music Awards (Moth & The Flame, n.d.).

Despite these successes, missed opportunities may abound for artists and brands alike if certain prospects are not considered at the outset.

"The particular problem with this [project] is we couldn't actually release the song," Lucy said, because "Follow Me" was commissioned by Airbnb as a custom song. "So it was a bit weird, because [...] at a moment when it's getting the most exposure you can't actually sell it or put it on Spotify."

Lucy's idea is one that brands are discovering themselves more and more, as is evident in the proliferation of branded Spotify pages, exclusive soundtracks, and more. There are many ways a brand can continue to leverage music from an ad long after the campaign concludes, especially if it includes owned music like Airbnb's "Follow Me" from Moth & The Flame.

"It was something I sort of wondered about. Could it happen where say we work with the brand to release it at the same time as exposure for both the company and the band?" said Lucy. "I think for bands it's not so much a monetary thing, because obviously you agreed to hand over the song. It's more about the exposure really."

For many artists, exposure is the greatest draw to music licensing. Record sales can no longer support artists as a primary source of revenue, which encouraged many to even upload their music for free in order to maximize exposure. Profits from touring have surpassed record sales. Even merchandise sales top it. Artists need loyal fans willing and eager to attend tours and shows; therefore, exposure is the preeminent recompense for almost any initiative an artist might take up. And the savvy artist will make the most of every piece of fan engagement.

"We notice [engagement] quite often when something gets used and it's on the internet," Lucy said. "Often people will ask, 'What's the name of the song?' and 'Who's this?' That's really nice to see, so we try and message people and pick up on that."

"I think as an artist now you have to do so much more yourself, and you sort of get used to having to do that sort of thing," Lucy continued. "If the brand can be a part of that as well, that's even better."

For the modern artist, this type of DIY engagement and social marketing is a paramount part of maximizing exposure and making the most of placements in ads, TV, film, and games. This is especially true for up-and-coming artists as they seek to gain a greater following. Additionally, Jason suggested considering licensing as an additional source of revenue as a means of supporting an artist's journey.

"The sensible thing would be to suggest thinking about the duality of the music," Jason said. "How can this work in terms of sync, how can this music work beyond just being a song for your band? Does it have any intrinsic value to a publisher, to a company like Music Dealers, or to a brand?"

"In 2010 I spent about two years touring around Europe with an artist. We were doing a lot of work and great shows, and in a sense it was kind of a dream gig for me," Jason said. "But I was writing for commercials and TV at the same time. In terms of workload vs income, that was far outweighing what you could earn from touring. And it was a well-paid touring job."

"But when those types of touring jobs finish, that's it," Jason said. "There's no money coming in from the market. It's not like you're going to continue getting the royalties from being on tour. I was working with a lot of different musicians at the time who were locked into that cycle, and it became increasingly obvious to me that you have two choices. You can either lock into that cycle of touring and get yourself involved in as many projects as you can, so when one tour ends you come in on the next one and the next one, and you end up like this one artist I worked with who was doing like 200 gigs each year. That's an insane amount of playing."

The other option is to do as Jason and Lucy did, and supplement their original passions with a revenue stream that still engaged them at their most creative level: music licensing. No longer perceived as selling out, music licensing is becoming increasingly lucrative for emerging artists, and a platform for discovery and as a generator of significant income. As consumers' interest in music grows, brands follow suit, and the marketing power of music increases the value of an authentic song that could engage a consumer accordingly.

"Music is the heart and soul of an audiovisual experience. How do you give depth to something you see, something that you look at?" said Jason. "It's the sound of music. I think the use of a song is just another deeper step into that process. Music and songs are so evocative, and it's such a powerful tool."

"As we get older as a human race, as a society, nostalgia becomes ever more prevalent," Jason said. "I think songs are sort of a perfect way to access that. Songs are all-powerful."

Airbnb Case Study

Sonic identity and Airbnb

Every marketer remembers the first advertisement that pulled her or him to the industry. For Jonathan Mildenhall, CMO of Airbnb and former content and marketing executive at Coca-Cola, one of the most notable components of that influential ad was its music.

In 1989, British Airways released its television commercial campaign, "Face," made by advertising firm Saatchi & Saatchi. Decades later, that spot is often considered a classic of television commercials. "Face" featured an adaptation by music composers Yanni and Malcolm McLaren of the famous song, "Flower Duet," originally written by the French composer Leo Delibes for his opera *Lakme* in the nineteenth century.

Over twenty-five years later, British Airways have since employed new slogans and campaigns; however, its music theme continues to represent the sonic identity of the brand. The "Flower Duet" is still used by the airlines in campaigns and on flights, and has been through several different arrangements since its original 1989 appearance.

"The relationship between music and narrative has always been a part of what makes amazing advertising," said Jonathan Mildenhall regarding the power of British Airlines' "Faces" campaign. "Music and story are so powerful [because] they are two of the first communication platforms that mankind [has] ever used. [...] Ancient man has always had a great relationship with story [because it's] the way that we learn, and a great relationship with music because it's the way we come together and express ourselves" (Mildenhall, 2015).

"When you put narrative and music together in advertising, you're hoping to build communities that understand the brand's ideology [...], [and are] inspired by the way the brand is expressing itself," continued Jonathan. "Ultimately, [music and story] come together to create really vibrant brands in the hearts and minds of consumers."

The recipient of numerous honors and awards, including "2012 AdAge Top 50 Creative People in Business," Jonathan knows good marketing when he sees it. Coca-Cola, Jonathan's previous employer, has long been a champion of using music to engage with consumers, a practice that Jonathan reportedly wanted to kickstart as soon as he joined the Airbnb team.

"At the time, I was only at Airbnb for literally four or five days before I put in the call to Music Dealers," said Jonathan regarding Airbnb's 2014 rebranding process. "First and foremost I wanted to add creative meaning to the company's new brand essence, which was this notion of belonging. Because of my own understanding of how music can travel around the world, [...] I actually wanted to use music as a lead storytelling platform for this new brand ideology, of which the world was [then] unaware. So, [we began] working with Music Dealers to basically develop musical anthems around this notion of belonging."

Through Music Dealers, Airbnb discovered Moth & The Flame. Music Dealers reached out to its artist community and delivered a short list of emerging artists whose sound aligned with the brand's new direction of belonging (as explored in the preceding case study with Lucy Underhill and Jason Tarver of Moth & The Flame). The Airbnb team analyzed that list and considered every aspect of the music, including such factors as lyrical quality, instrumental components, and even the biographies of the artists. This due diligence led to a discovery that cemented the relationship between Moth & The Flame and Airbnb.

After researching the stories of the several artists Music Dealers presented to Airbnb, the team found that Lucy and Jason were indeed part of their own community of travelers who used Airbnb during their travels. Though emerging artists are obviously not the only users of the accommodations site, the authentic relationship between Moth & The Flame and Airbnb emerged because of the sporadic touring and recording schedules of Lucy and Tarver. Few demographics travel as much as artists do, thus revealing to the brand an entirely fresh angle that could not have been accessed had a sound designer, agency, or marketing company created the music for the "Belong Anywhere" campaign.

"What was particularly interesting about Moth & The Flame is they're already part of our community," said Jonathan. "They travel on Airbnb and when they travel on Airbnb, they're putting their homes on Airbnb. So there was such an authentic and organic fit with that particular band, with their story that they wrote about belonging, and [with] the musical melody that went on [to] travel around the world."

After setting their sights on Moth & The Flame, Airbnb began working with Lucy and Jason to record the song and then applied it across multiple touchpoints, including a web video, a landing page, and even a live performance. This comprehensive application of music by Airbnb hit at the three key functions of music strategy – attraction, immersion, and extension – in such a powerful way that the campaign became the most widely traveled piece of content that, at that point, Airbnb had created, according to Jonathan. News stories in reference to Moth & The Flame work appeared, according to Jonathan, in 182 countries after the campaign launched, which is even more noteworthy considering the brand was only in 191 countries. Through authentic music Airbnb attracted consumers' attention, immersed them into the new brand, and extended the relationship between the brand and the consumer beyond the lodging experience. Moth & The Flame had spread the brand's new sense of belonging faster and further than traditional advertising could ever on its own.

"Music travels further than any other genre of content or branding statement," said Jonathan. "Music travels further and quicker than advertising. Music travels further and quicker than film. Music travels further and quicker than print. Music travels further and quicker than merchandising."

Music travels further than any other genre of content or branding statement

"Music is, to use a Coke terminology, the most liquid of content platforms," continued Jonathan. "So when you're a small company but you're all over the world, which is what Airbnb was, we use music as a way of uniting our communities, [which] are in 191 countries."

After the "Belong Anywhere" rebrand campaign first ran, music continues to play a large role in the brand's marketing strategy, Jonathan expressed. For example, as the world recognized the 25th anniversary of the fall of the Berlin Wall in 2015, Airbnb contributed to the global celebration with its moving video "Wall and Chain," the music in which helps communicate this uniquely inspiring campaign.

A tale only possible through Airbnb, the story of three German citizens whose lives were inexorably linked to the Wall – Jörg, Cathrine, and Kai – captivates viewers as they demonstrate the liberties that belonging anywhere affords. Just as the cadence of "Follow Me" by Moth & The Flame represented the sound of the new Airbnb logo, the Bélo, the brand sought another custom song that could represent that same sonic identity of belonging anywhere for "Wall and Chain" (Music Dealers, n.d.).

Under the direction of the Airbnb marketing content team, the brand decided to craft an animated adaptation of Jörg's story rather than feature live actors in order to increase the universality of the story's message, as reported on the Music Dealers website. Similarly, as production company Psyop developed the "Wall and Chain" film, Airbnb contacted Music Dealers to discover an evocative song that could break through barriers in its own right and match the emotional power of the spot.

Just as the inspiring story of Cathrine, Kai, and Jörg is unique, the film required a distinctive sound constructed specially for the campaign. Music Dealers Creative Director Tim Lincoln sourced the company's global community of independent artists and, in the same vein as the "Belong Anywhere" campaign, briefed them on the song requirements to create a custom composition that could aptly express the tenderness of the spot. After reviewing the submissions, Airbnb decided on "Petit Oiseau" by Austin-based composer, Nick Seeley.

An emotional campaign that encourages viewers to break down barriers of all kinds, "Wall and Chain" builds brand awareness by promoting the company's message of belonging anywhere. In less than a week, the video garnered 2,300,000 views on YouTube, over 2,000 favorites on Twitter, and over 250,000 views on Facebook. With the gentle cadence of Nick Seeley's "Petit Oiseau," music helped extend Jörg's story – and the strong brand of Airbnb – with the world (Wall and Chain, n.d.).

"I think clever marketers use music as a strategic platform, because if they use music right, it travels further and helps accelerate the speed with which other forms of content travel," said Jonathan, speaking on the ubiquity of music over other mediums. "[Music] connects deeper than anything else, which is why it travels, and as a result of that deeper connection, it recalls longer than anything else."

Though Airbnb has swiftly grown into a global powerhouse – *The Wall Street Journal*'s "Billion Dollar Startup Club" of companies valued at $1 billion or more by venture-capital firms – ranked Airbnb as the 3rd highest valued startup, as of August 2015 – it is still a considerably young, and therefore developing, brand (Scott Austin, n.d.). All startups can probably attest to the difficult balancing act between spreading your brand as far and wide as possible, yet at the same time hone a specific, brand persona. In the world of modern marketing, wherein social and emerging media can allow for a range of mass distribution of branded content, it is part of the role of the modern marketer to conceptualize and implement a means by which all activity can be reined into one cohesive brand identity.

A quick glance at Jonathan's experience in adland, from Account Director at BBH to CMO of Airbnb, reveals at least two unfailing brand tactics: music and storytelling.

"I have as wide of an application for music as I have for storytelling. I think great stories create better marketing [and] great music creates better marketing," said Jonathan regarding the wide range of ways that Airbnb incorporates both throughout their messaging.

"Airbnb has always had a very progressive outlook on marketing. In fact, the music and video team were established at Airbnb before the advertising team," said Jonathan. "Airbnb's marketing muscle was originally designed on experiential marketing, because we actually couldn't afford traditional advertising. So, when we used to show up in places like Sundance and South by Southwest and [created] these amazing experiences, we knew music was going to be one of the core parts of making [these] very special Airbnb experiences come to life."

As reported by many adland pundits, experiential marketing is rapidly becoming a favored alternative to traditional advertising, though concrete metrics for its ROI are as murky as its definition. Sometimes defined as messaging consumers can touch, feel, or view in the physical space, other times simply defined as a form of advertising that focuses primarily on helping consumers experience a brand, experiential marketing is an attractive yet elusive strategy for the modern marketer.

As explained in this section, music could become a widely applied solution to customer experience for many brands who are struggling to connect ROI, customer experience, and brand integrity. Naturally emotive, music can be composed or curated to create a sonic identity that ties any messaging – from experiential marketing to traditional advertising – back to the overarching brand. As a passion point with intrinsic value for consumers, music can provide the diving board from which consumers can immerse themselves into the story of the brand. As an inherently experiential medium, brands can partner with artists to create engaging activations that extend the B2C relationship long after the product experience.

The San Francisco-based startup whose radically novel model raised eyebrows industry wide, Airbnb has since driven its valuation past some of the largest publicly traded hotel chains. Guiding millions along the customer journey with its expansive music strategy was one of several factors that has facilitated their ascension.

"When people travel, they listen to music more than when they're at home," said Jonathan on the importance of music to the Airbnb brand. "The relationship people have with music and travel is a really deep relationship. [...] Music as a content platform in the context of travel is arguably more important to me now than it was in my last position."

"But now I would always want to make sure that the content could be applied anywhere, [and] one of the pieces of content would be an unplugged performance of that content in and around a great Airbnb listing," said Jonathan, demonstrating the depth of influence music can play in a brand's marketing strategy if only marketers decide to leverage it.

"Very progressive marketing organizations actually have music talent within the marketing department itself," said Jonathan. "I don't mean composers or performers, I mean people who have actually studied music or come from the music industry. They basically become the conduit for the brand and for organizations like Music Dealers to create amazing content that engages in a very deep and profound way with our target audiences."

On a personal note, I've yet to meet anyone who has pushed me to never settle for anything but absolute perfection the way Jonathan has. He's always been a model I've looked to when asking myself, "Is this good enough?" He pushes everyone on his team to be their best, and it results in award-winning work, content people want to share, and a personal sense of accomplishment most people would never reach without his determination.

This hustle is the bedrock of successful campaigns like "Belong Anywhere," "Wall and Chain," and Airbnb's marketing strategy as a whole. Students of any industry would be wise to take note of Jonathan's testimonial, and look to these projects as inspiration in the same way that he regarded "Face" by British Airways.

No Wyld Artist Success Story

Shortly before indie-pop hit Lorde brought international attention to her native country of New Zealand, three Kiwis came together while attending the University of Auckland to form a band whose sound was unique to both New Zealand and the globe.

No Wyld, formerly known as The Wyld, blends hip-hop, electro-pop, and blues-rock through what the band has described as a "sonic alchemy" of musical influences. Comprised of rapper Mo Kheir, singer and keyboardist Brandon Black, and guitarist Joe Pascoe, No Wyld formed following an electronic music jam night hosted by fellow Auckland outfit Jupiter Project, according to *The New Zealand Herald* (Kara, 2012).

In five short years, No Wyld ascended the steps to the global stage, evolving their signature sound into an anthemic call-to-action that wooed fans and brands alike.

The band's first single, "Revolution," from their first album, *Preface* (2012), helped spread the band across the internet world via notable blogs like MTV Iggy, Pigeons & Planes, and Cassette Couture. The song was subsequently synced to *90210*, encouraging the trio to head back to the studio for another recording session that would lead to one of the band's greatest milestones to date.

Abstract was released in late 2013 and spread like quiet wildfire from Auckland to indie-tuned ears everywhere, including Music Dealers.

"This the type of song you don't see on TV/ We major and minor your highness/ We can tell you're scared not feeling our flyness/ No risk taken by A&R chasers/ All they want is pop tracks for ad placements," raps Kheir on the track, "Walk Away," from their EP, *Abstract*.

Despite the obstinate tone of the last two lines, the A&R and creative teams at Music Dealers fell in love with the EP, especially the track "Odyssey." In no time at all, they found the perfect ad placement to escalate the band to global fame.

Following a Sonic Identity Workshop with McDonald's and DDB, in which we helped McDonald's craft a musical style guide and determine how to better apply music in future projects, the three entities – McDonald's, DDB, and Music Dealers – collaborated for the brand's 2014 Olympics spot, "Celebrate with a Bite." The video features footage from past Olympic games, amassing to a kaleidoscopic film ripe with nostalgia and pride. To guarantee the right emotional response, Music Dealers pitched "Odyssey" by The Wyld, stunning the client with the strong compatibility of this selection (Music Dealers, n.d.).

In order to build a stronger connection with its audience of highly musically-oriented consumers, McDonald's, official sponsor of the Olympics, decided to incorporate music more in its campaign for the 2014 games than in previous placements. For the brand's spearhead commercial of the event, "Celebrate with a Bite," McDonald's sought a song that worked with the video to incur a genuine emotional response from viewers and to generate enthusiasm for the games.

Initially, DDB creatives searched "Beautiful Piano" in our company catalog and selected a delicate, sentimental piano piece for the spot; before the deal could be finalized, however, Music Dealers Creative Director Jessie LaBelle suggested "Odyssey" by No Wyld, a song with a deep timbre and a driving, dynamic beat. Jessie pulled the vocals from the track and synced the instrumentals with the video, creating a memorable masterpiece.

By complementing the nostalgia of the "Celebrate with a Bite" spot with The Wyld's momentous rhythm of "Odyssey," expert music supervision elevated the emotional impact of the McDonald's campaign through the unexpected energy that effused from the commercial. The whole campaign for McDonald's evolved through the spot, directly because of the brand's leveraging of new, independent music to cultivate a unique sound that genuinely connected with viewers.

Marketing Week called the campaign "a global push to introduce its 'unofficial anthem' for the Winter Olympics and usher in a new way of connecting with its fans through music" (Joseph, 2014). According to *AdWeek*'s Lost Remote blog, the spot was the most searched ad on Google, Bing, and Yahoo! for the Olympics, and generated just under 500,000 searches within minutes of airing (Flomenbaum, 2014).

"Since we first started putting up music to blogs, we thought our music was cinematic and it would fit in film and television and things like that. And that was something we were always pretty open to," said Joe Pascoe. "We were very aware that it was another avenue for exposure, a chance to earn some money for our music, and [...] to have people hear you" (Pascoe, 2015).

Immediately following the release of *Abstract*, the band's manager began pitching their music to a few different people. Once it reached our ears at Music Dealers, the music was fast-tracked through the review process and swiftly uploaded into our catalog of music. Shortly after, McDonald's and DDB Chicago came to us with the brief for "Celebrate With A Bite."

"Once we found out it was really tied in with The Olympics as well, and that it was going to be quite a large campaign, we were very interested, and got quite excited," continued Joe. "And then we saw the rough edit of the ad and we were really glad it worked out."

According to McDonald's research, the campaign drove Chicken McNugget sales up 18% over a declining baseline. But not only did the spot gain the brand international attention and an incredible ROI on their campaign, it also catapulted No Wyld into the next stage of their music career.

"The ad ran two weeks for the Olympics, and for the first week, we were the most viral track in the world on Spotify because of the ad placement," said Joe. "And in the second week we were the second most viral track in the world. And both of those weeks, if you looked at the top ten most viral tracks of the world, we were the only act that was completely independent, not signed to any major or minor label. So from that point we just started getting bombarded by labels."

"From there we got a lot of offers to come and play in the States. So we got some money together and we came over and played the shows. I think we played maybe five or six shows on the East and West coasts. And off the back of those shows, from the sales numbers that we did off the back of the ad, and just from the exposure and the things that we'd had, we signed with Columbia Records."

The trajectory of No Wyld's career – from three university students jamming together to an international hit – is indicative of the evolving music industry. What it means to be an artist nowadays is a very different model than in previous generations, with very different milestones of success, and with a very different perspective on brand partnerships.

"We come from a different type of generation," said Joe. "Our music discovery comes from placements on TV shows and ads, so that's not seen in the same negative light that it was maybe viewed in the past. And it's so easy now, with Shazam and stuff, to find out what song was on the ad. You might not like the ad, but you might still love the song."

Artists like No Wyld aren't the only ones picking up on this new trend. More and more, brands are reaching out to artists to create advertisements and campaigns that access the artists' creativity and fanbase to craft targeted brand positioning and messaging.

"Now, though, [brands] are realizing there's actually a lot of marketing to be gained by associating positively with these artists rather than just using them for their chain or whatever," said Joe. "So I think we'll see a lot more expended for music, like how Beats by Dre really works with artists and really develops and fosters relationships. I think that will be a lot more common, especially for big brands."

"I definitely would always recommend to an artist to be open to syncs and licenses. And I think most are now, I haven't talked to an artist lately that has said anything negative about it. Everyone's trying to get their career going and everyone realizes there's good money there, and it can be really good exposure."

No Wyld is a clear example of how licensing can be that added avenue for exposure that can catapult the career of an up-and-coming artist. As soon as their single "Queen" was released from their then yet-to-be-released album, it was picked up by Apple and HBO to advertise the brands' joint streaming platform, HBO Now.

"Queen" is reminiscent of the driving quality that made *Abstract* such a powerful EP, yet its refined sound shows how the band has progressed with their success in their five short years since forming. According to Joe, media like television and film have had an influence on that sound.

"We watch a lot of movies and we watch a lot of TV, like a lot of people our age too, and our musical taste is influenced by what we hear all the time," said Joe. "Some of that really cinematic sound definitely crept into our work, and I think that definitely helps with syncs and placements. But that's not why we do it. It's more our musical tastes, the tastes of the general public, and everything just starting to meld a lot more."

"There's been a number of times when one of us has made a piece of music and then sat down with it, and thought like, 'Man that sounds like it could be on the trailer for the new *Batman* film or something like that.' We don't sit there and say, 'Let's write this song and try and get it on *Batman*,'" said Joe, though he admitted licensing "is definitely on our minds."

"Getting like a placement in a movie would be awesome. Something like a Marvel movie trailer or something like that, that's always something that we want to do," said Joe. "We wouldn't get our music placed anywhere that we wouldn't be proud to have it placed. So any placements that we get, we're really proud to tell people that we've gotten them and to go check them out."

For a band whose fanbase spread via trending blogs like Pigeons & Planes and Cassette Couture, that type of brand advocacy can mean a world of difference to the culturally minded modern consumer. As artists continue to have greater communication with their fanbase, like No Wyld does, brands should increase their efforts to partner with these artists to hit their consumers hardest.

"It's obviously very important to have people who are culturally influential," said Joe. "And musicians and actors seem to have the largest cultural influence, at least to the general consumer, so it just makes sense."

After all, Chicken McNuggets don't sell themselves. Music does.

DDB Chicago, Company Spotlight

It's hard to look at the body of work of Jean Batthany, Executive Creative Director and EVP of the advertising agency DDB Chicago, and not be impressed. Kohler, American Cancer Society, British Airways, and Arby's are only a few of the brands that Jean helped build. Couple that with two back-to-back awards – Advertising Working Mothers of the Year 2015 and The 30 Most Creative Women in Advertising 2015 – and you've got a whole creative dream-team crammed into one mighty brain.

Throughout Jean's work, the common creative thread that links them all is her commitment to providing consumers with content they can care about, that has intrinsic value to it beyond just product-pushing. Music is a frequent tool in Jean's wheelhouse that she and the DDB Chicago team leverage in order to fulfill consumer expectations for quality communications.

"Way back in the day, I saw the ad business as purely convincing people to buy what they did not want or need," said Jean in an email interview. "Advertising is certainly the art of persuasion, designed to shape and influence the perceptions of the public. But it is also a powerful change agent, trendsetter, and entertainment vehicle. The modern consumer is exposed to so many messages every day. Thus they wield an incredible amount of power and demand more from brands in exchange for their loyalty ... more relevance, more entertainment, and more purpose" (Batthany, 2015).

Jean has worked at a variety of shops after graduating from FIT, working on a range of projects before moving to DDB in 2012, a renowned agency whose global network took home 78 Lions from the 2015 Cannes Lions International Festival of Creativity (DDB Worldwide, n.d.). Some of the DDB network's notable campaigns, beyond its

McDonald's "Celebrate With A Bite" project, include the branded content for "Monty the Penguin" and the integrated campaign for "The Bear and the Hare," both of which were holiday campaigns for the UK brand, John Lewis. These Christmas advertisements are globally anticipated for their phenomenal use of music, an area that Jean has watched grow in the industry over the years of her expertise.

"When I first started, a lot more original music was being scored with live performers with real instruments, even orchestras. God help us, the jingle was still alive and well," said Jean. "But things got very synthesized very fast. At the time, relevant pop and rock stars wouldn't be caught dead licensing their music to shill for a brand as it was seen as selling out."

"But then there was definitely a cultural shift and you started hearing songs from bands old and new on commercials. I spent a lot of time at BBDO in the Pepsi days where music played a huge role. Everything from mega pop stars like Michael Jackson to oldies but goodies were negotiated in an attempt to create a culture of cool. Definitely a more expensive option than scoring an original piece, but instantly recognizable tracks reduced risk and brought instant social currency. Now it's commonplace, and for up-and-coming artists it can be seen as a vehicle for success and sales. Apple really changed the way advertising could make a song or band explode with their cool cult status. Creatives everywhere were and still are trying to capture that magic."

As Jean expressed, "selling out" has become a thing of the past for artists, both established and emerging. Because of the reach that brands have, artists are looking at advertisements and branded campaigns as an opportunity for exposure, revenue, and for creative collaboration, too. The content that some of the world's top brands are producing through agencies like DDB are also some of the most evocative pieces of short film, be they the holiday adverts of John Lewis or empowering spots like Dove's now iconic "Like A Girl" campaign.

The range of music strategy that a brand employs depends on several factors, too. Perusing the credits of any one commercial reveals many teams working together, from agencies to post-production houses to music agencies like Music Dealers, and more.

"Both the size and attitude of the agency, as well as clients, are reflected in the music approach. Some agencies invest in an in-house music producer, who is potentially more knowledgeable and more connected to the music scene than the average creative. And some clients just have deeper pockets and want the star power that comes along with a known track while others don't see the value."

Regardless of the size of a brand or the scale of a campaign, music in advertising follows the same guidelines of music strategy, as outlined in this book. Music and sound can accomplish a great many feats, or, depending on the client, it might not be valued as a high-priority part of the puzzle. Unfortunately, lost opportunities to attract, immerse, and extend consumer experiences through music occur far too often, especially when there's not an in-house music executive in an agency or if a music agency is not brought in to consult on music strategy.

In any project, the ultimate goal is of course to support the content; however, the ultimate goal of the content is to guide viewers along the consumer journey. If strong music strategy can accomplish both, then it would seem obvious to leverage it.

"Some creatives will have a very strong point of view for either the direction of music or a song when they share a concept," said Jean. "Especially if music is integral to the idea or will affect how we shoot or edit. Sometimes we'll put tracks against rips as we sell work through, which can be dangerous if it's well-known and potentially unattainable due to budget or talent as it runs the risk of demo love with the client. During the production process, the director, editor, and clients all tend to have strong opinions about music and it can be an extremely collaborative process. Sometimes we end up in a long-drawn-out search and others you find and hear 'the one' right off."

There is no silver bullet solution to music strategy and supervision; as will be reiterated several times throughout this book, music supervision is an art and cannot therefore be replicated at will. As Jean explained, the search for the right song can go a number of ways, especially when some creatives have a strong opinion on the direction of music. While some may say this is just having too many cooks in the kitchen, the more invested creatives are in the music direction of a campaign, even if they themselves won't be supervising the music licensing and sync of the project, the better. As long as they appreciate the musical expertise of those who are on the other end of the soundboard, it can be a powerful thing to have a team full of creatives who have a strong investment in the music of a campaign. Those are the champions of music strategy in advertising agencies, as they will be the ones pushing for higher music budgets and more involved music campaigns.

One of DDB's clients, Kohler, has begun implementing music strategy more and more into its marketing, such as its "Shower Out Loud" campaign at Bonnaroo festival in 2015 and its ad, "Never Too Timeless." In the latter case, the song that was synced to the spot, "Black Magic Boy" by Fran Hall, earned 3,500+ listens on Spotify in its first three months after the ad aired and was made available for purchase on iTunes.

"As we launched the Never Too Platform with Kohler, we really wanted to partner with up-and-coming artists and influencers, across all mediums that embodied the spirit of the campaign and the brand to live beyond the normal," explained Jean.

"As we were producing the 'Timeless' spot, Creative Directors Nathan Monteith and Andrew Bloom found a very cool clubby track from Australian producer and DJ Alison Wonderland via Nowness. The clients weren't 100% sold, so we parallel-pathed music approaches.

We asked the team at Massive Music to score an original track to our final cut, and Music Dealers was brought in to search for an existing track from an indie band that would marry well with the edit. MD sent us many, including "Black Magic Boy" by Fran Hall, which had both a vintage and modern sound and married extremely well with the visual story of traveling through time."

The captivating "Never TOO Timeless" spot guides viewers on a glitzy jaunt through the bathrooms of the Victorian era, to the Art Deco days, to the iconic '50s, and finally to contemporary times. Set to the jazzy beat of "Black Magic Boy," the campaign celebrates the specialist, design roots of the brand with this artistic ad. The spot earned 2.5+ million views on YouTube in its first three months, culminating in two years of viewership in only twelve weeks ("Never TOO Timeless," n.d.). Furthermore, Fran Hall was asked to speak at ASCAP's 10th annual "I Create Music" expo in May because of her successful songwriting career and her experience with projects like "Never TOO Timeless" (Music Dealers, n.d.).

The "Never TOO Timeless" campaign is a strong example of how an ad whose focus is the visual story rather than the song can nonetheless incorporate a strong music strategy in order to maximize the marketing power of music. The song was artfully crafted by an emerging artist and attracted many eyes and ears to the spot during the commercial, and immersed viewers into the sonic identity of the brand by matching the personality of Kohler. Additionally, the song was uploaded online to extend the consumer relationship with the brand through the music even after the ad stopped airing.

"Getting it up on iTunes was a no-brainer as people were asking what the song was as soon as the commercial was posted on YouTube, where it's up to 2.5+ million views," said Jean.

Kohler was also a sponsor of Bonnaroo in 2015 and executed several music activations around it, including Spotify playlists, Instagram campaigns, and onsite activities to feature its Moxie showerhead, which incorporated music strategy so deeply into its design that the product delivers up to 7 hours of music through a wireless speaker in the sprayface (Kohler, n.d.). According to Jean, there were many creative partners involved in the Bonnaroo campaign, including Revolver Media, Complex, Spotify, Pandora, and social influencers at the festival, as well as Kohler's own extensive internal creative and marketing team.

"We definitely felt the NEVER TOO brand platform aligned extremely well with the partnership and thus were all for it. Collectively we saw it as a cool and authentic place to connect with a younger audience and the Moxie bluetooth showerhead the perfect product to demo Kohler's attitude and innovation to very dirty music + tech-loving millennials. Sort of a gateway drug if you will to the Kohler brand with an accessible price point," said Jean.

Early in the interview, Jean commented on what most excites me about the evolution of advertising. No longer is it an industry that's out to "convince people to buy what they don't want or need." When done right, advertising can be a change agent, a trendsetter, an entertainment vehicle. The differentiating factor between the two pathways is truly enriching the lives of consumers and, as Jean said, making them feel something authentic. Music isn't the only route to emotive advertising, but as the world's most shared passion, it can definitely be the fastest and most powerful way of building a real bond between brands and consumers.

Sonixphere, Company Spotlight

Music in media is a complex, evolving industry – as is suggested in the demand for a book like *Return of the Hustle* on the subject. Audio branding is one of the key components of that construct. Audio branding, sonic identity, and music strategy interweave like currents in a river: sometimes they overlap, sometimes they intersect, and sometimes they are so concurrent that they seem as if one.

Greg Allan is a prominent name in the field of audio branding, and worked to discover the ubiquitous yet mysterious "sound of the brand" for numerous companies over the years, including the sound of Bud Light's "Drinkability" and McDonald's "Little Fishy Fishy" campaign.

According to Greg, his journey began like many in this industry – a love for music.

"I think a lot of us were in bands back in the day," Greg said during an interview in the Sonixphere office. "For one reason or another, it doesn't work, so you kind of go, 'OK, where else can I use my talents?'" (Allan, 2015)

The music industry was never an inclusive space, at least not for the wildly successful. Over the years, however, that small gap at the top of the industry of the rich and famous began to shrink. Fewer stars were made, but the general adoration of music continued to thrive. Music's role in society was as powerful as ever – if not more. Therefore, more spaces for artists and music lovers slowly began to grow.

Music for brands was one such area. As technology proliferated and allowed for sound and audio experimentation, greater opportunities for music in media grew. In the 1980s, jingles – a short slogan, verse, or tune that is easily remembered and is custom to a brand – were at their peak in popularity. Greg earned his first opportunity in this space and excelled, beginning as a staff composer and eventually forging his way to co-owner of Spank! Music & Sound Design, which he worked with for nearly fifteen years. Since then, Greg has formed a new original music company called Sonixphere in Chicago and is also a partner at the sound design company, STIR Post.

Like everyone in the music industry, Greg has seen a lot of change. The evolution of music in media happened for a number of reasons, and it will continue to adapt to fit consumer demands and trends. Only those who discover how to blend the successes of the past with innovations of the present will survive the perpetual shifts of the music industry's growth.

"All along, we had been doing mnemonics," Greg explains. "They were called mnemonics, or a tag, and we had to write very very catchy, between four- and seven-note hooks. It's amazing how much power that has, and it still works. I mean, bad-dah bah-bah-bah [the McDonald's mnemonic] is still one of the most recognizable mnemonics there are."

"Some brands got away from it as time went on," Greg continued. "But we still do them, all the time. Some of them did become sound design, and that was because maybe the brand changed its image and it was no longer about notes as much as it was 'what's the sound of the brand?' And that's what audio branding is."

The definition of audio branding is as fickle as the industry that gave birth to it. In this book, we define Audio Branding as the process by which a brand – in any industry, including television, film, and gaming, too – builds its sonic identity through the use of audio logos and branded sounds. Audio branding and music strategy operate together to build a brand's sonic identity, and often overlap – in fact, when the two converge and the brand's music strategy responds to the audio branding, the brand's sonic identity is strongest. Because most individuals in the advertising and branding space are not cut of the same sonic cloth of many in the music space, it can be difficult to narrow down what is a brand's sonic identity.

"So, what is the sound of your brand?" Greg postulated. "If you ask a brand manager or someone who's up in that echelon of people, some of them will know and most won't. And that's where our job comes in."

The process by which the sound of a brand is discovered varies from job to job, and of course from industry to industry; however, there are certain steps that Greg follows each time.

"You want to know as much as you can know about the brand," said Greg. "You want to know who their target is, what age are they, what ethnicity are they. If it's really pinpointed, then it's a little easier. If it's wide open, that's tougher. [...] You have to figure out how to wrangle in some more info. So maybe we'll get some information from some of the labels on what that age group is listening to and things like that. They [the record labels] have all the info you could possibly ever need."

"You sort of go, 'OK, well here's the target you're looking for, here's what they're listening to. OK, but where are they going to be?' Like Dubstep. As fast as it came, it's almost gone," Greg continued. "You're not going to audio brand a company based on a sound that's happening right this second that's probably going to go away. It's got to have longevity to it."

Longevity is a key component of sonic identity. In the same way that a brand's logo or character should endure the test of time, its sonic identity should be crafted to persist through changing landscapes of music, technology, and culture.

Longevity is a key component of sonic identity

Though music trends are one of the most fickle phenomena in culture, a brand can indeed leverage music strategy in its marketing and still maintain relevancy. It begins with the character of the brand. All marketers consider this, and each campaign, advertisement, and market reposition begins with understanding the character, or sometimes called the moral identity, of the brand. If the brand was a person, who would that person be? What would she stand for? How would she interact with others?

And what would her music tastes be?

Proper music strategy begins with the understanding that people change their music interests as often as music trends change; however, that doesn't preclude a long-term music strategy. Though an individual – a real, live person – may stream The Weeknd's new release on repeat one week and never listen to it again, that person's music identity is still her own. When she goes to a psych-rock fest a month later, she'll still be the same person who had dug The Weeknd weeks prior.

The soundtrack to her life may have changed, but her sonic identity remained. The songs on her Spotify page have been updated, but the rationale behind their curation persists into the next playlist. Brands need to do the same in order to build a strong sonic identity through music – not necessarily stick to one genre, because, as Greg noted, genres come and go. Marketers need to develop the musical side of their brand's character and feature music that accurately fits the mold.

The other side of sonic identity – audio branding – requires just as much care in order to guarantee a sound with longevity.

"It's a big deal," Greg said. "We put a ton of time into audio branding. [...] We ask a lot of questions, we have internal meetings about the sound of it. [...] We all get together and brainstorm. [...] Where will it be in five years or three years? [...] A lot of thought goes into it, before we even write a note. Once we do, that's where all collectively write or create sounds or whatever. And we don't just go to a synth and pick a sound. It's all built. It's never a stock sound."

"There's no one way in particular," Greg continued. "The one thing for sure is, we always go back to the same question, which is, 'What is the sound of your brand?' And that is more than fifty percent of the work. [...] It's all creative, but it's much more thinking on the front-end. It's not sitting down with a piano [or] just coming up with a great drum loop or coming up with a great groove. And once you figure out what the sound of that brand [is], then you take it to the next level and be more creative knowing that this is my palette of sounds for this brand."

That sonic palette is the range of sounds that define the audio-branded component of a brand's sonic identity. Tone, pitch, instrument, and more all contribute to that sonic palette, which can then be mixed, sampled, and arranged, much like an artist's palette of paint, Greg said. And in the same way that painters look at colors as either warm or cold, intense or gentle, Greg and his team select the sounds of the brand according to the emotional qualities of those sounds in relation to the brand's character. For example, Greg described one project due to rollout in 2016 that the team recently developed for an upcoming line of automobiles. The audio brand begins with "an impactful sound that says that they're a leader, and it's followed by a very warm and pointed three-note succession to show they care."

This process echoes the means by which music strategy is developed to reflect the character of the brand. Songs can be searched and stored according to hundreds of different types of filters. To help bring this type of strategy expertise to ad creatives and supervisors, the way I developed the organization of the Music Dealers catalog is according to moods that range from uneasy to naughty, vocal themes that range from day-dreaming to revolution, and more tags of similar variety. A brand can create a palette of music and a palette of sounds in its quest for a strong sonic identity by which to brand its character.

For example, Greg and his team worked on the documentary television series *Flying Wild Alaska*, which aired on Discovery Channel for three seasons in 2011 and 2012. According to Greg, few reality TV shows invest in proper audio branding – "You know it's always overdo everything. Overdo the strings for the crying section, overdo the comedy for the quirky things and stuff like that" – but *Flying Wild Alaska* decided that a strong sonic identity was important for the story.

"We worked with Doug Bossi at iSpy, and Doug said, 'We need to find the sound of the show,'" Greg said. "And so I said, 'OK, let's approach this like when we brand for brands.' So, knowing that it was in Alaska, we went the obvious way and did our homework on music from that territory. That seemed like too straight up the aisle. Anybody could do that, you know. [...] So we decided, 'You know what, let's try to find some unusual instrumentation.' Or even if it's not unusual, maybe it's unusual for the show. In other words, it could've been a solo violin, which would've been weird for these rugged shots of Alaska, but how does that work, how does that pull us into the show? [...] That [...] didn't really answer all the questions that we had posed to ourselves at the time." Greg was concentrating on how to achieve maximum immersion with these unique ideas to pull viewers into the show.

"So, we went through multiple rounds of trying to find the sound of the show, and a lot of the sound of the show is this kind of pulse," Greg continued. "There's kind of a tension, but it's not like that typical reality tension. There's a pulse that goes through, [...] this kind of underlying pulse, as they're setting up to go fly and it could go down at any point. And it wasn't overbearing. [...] [But] what kind of sound are we going to create with that? So, in the end, after trying probably fifty different instruments, we settled on a baritone guitar, which is right over there [points in his office]. It was an eerie feel to it. It has a low tone to it. A lot of the frequencies of the show are the plane, and they're all in this high frequency range. So everything that we were writing was competing with the sounds of the show. [...] It works well as part of the pulse."

"And then from there, you end up writing hundreds of cues for the show, and they all revolve around the sound of the show," Greg continued. "So that was well-branded. Well-branded. And then obviously the theme."

"Frozen Sky," according to Greg, was created based off of the audio brand of the show that they had developed through the pairing of the baritone guitar with the resonant pulse of the show. The team mixed orchestral instruments, native Alaskan percussion, and contemporary instrumentation to capture the danger of being a pilot in the rough conditions of Alaska, as the Sonixphere site explains (Sonixphere, n.d.).

Additionally, production collaborated with the rapper Peand-eL, a native of Greenland who released the single, "Takoqqarnert" (First Time I Saw You) around the time the show aired in 2011 when his popularity was highest. The show also featured a number of other Native artists, including Greenlandic artists Kimmernaq, TuuMotz, and Nanook, as well as Alaskan artists Pamyua and Frozen Whitefish. Furthermore, the music from the show is available on iTunes, which extended the relationship between viewer and show even more (Meigs, 2011).

Through the music strategy that followed Greg's central theme song, "Frozen Sky," maintained the solid sonic identity that he and his team helped craft, which attracted viewers back each week, immersed them in the experience by debuting new songs, and extended the conversations by having viewers talk about and share the songs featured in the programing. It's extra work to research and discover authentic, local musicians, and to then find ways to incorporate them into the show, but putting in that extra effort creates new touchpoints and ways for viewers to engage with the show. Beyond that immersion during the show, this strategy gives viewers reasons to talk about the show with friends and share the music he helped them discover. In doing so, Greg didn't just help create loyal viewers; the convergence of audio branding and music strategy created advocates and turned viewers into promoters by unleashing the marketing power of music.

If a tree falls in a forest when no one's around to hear it, does it even make a sound? If a brand creates an audio brand and doesn't leverage it across any audio touchpoints, does it even have a sound?

After discovering the sound of the brand, an important but overlooked step in audio branding is deciding where, when, and how to repurpose those "sonic nuggets," as Greg calls them. In this book, we call all of those various places audio touchpoints, which are any place – whether physical or virtual, static or dynamic – wherein the brand interacts with its consumers that does or may involve sound.

Creating a branded sound – whether through music strategy, sound design or audio branding – does nothing to increase engagement with consumers if that sound is never heard. As explored in this book, there are numerous (perhaps innumerable) audio touchpoints that a brand can access to connect with its audiences. Not every audio touchpoint will be wholly relevant to every brand; however, the more a brand does leverage (and the better job they do of it, too), then the stronger of a sonic identity they will establish with their consumers.

"Audio branding is not just the tag," said Greg. "Audio branding really should be [...] an audio branding palette of sounds. So maybe it's something that lives in a kiosk somewhere, or it's online somewhere, or there's no form attached to it anywhere."

"Like Coors Light," Greg continued. "They had the Silver Bullet [campaign] and had The O'Jays' song, 'Love Train.' There was a blue tint that would go over the mountain. That right there should've been audio branded to sound, their sound. [...] So now all of a sudden we would have the train sound, which should have been created and not just regular sound effects – sound designed. Maybe it's a song that targets the 20-year-old that they're trying to go after. And maybe the blue tint has its own sound. Now maybe in a store somewhere they have something more experiential where they grab a beer can and it has the freezing sound." No matter which direction they could have gone, Greg points out that there were places they could have immersed the viewer into the visuals more with proper and deliberate music strategy.

"I mean there is so much you could've done with that. That's all part of audio branding. It's not just what's happening at the end of the commercial. It's what sound palette are we going to use for this brand everywhere."

While there are truly millions of places people are hearing and listening to sounds, there is a delicate balance between crafting a comprehensive audio branding strategy and creating simply a whole lot of noise pollution. Sound pollution, Greg explained, can be described in the example of the customary shopping center: air conditioners blowing, various voices ringing across intercoms, multiple music tracks playing in different parts of the store, TVs and electronics buzzing in dissonance, and consumers echoing that chaos throughout their shopping experience from walk-in to check-out.

"It's literally a sonic nightmare," Greg said with a sigh.

There is no easy way to navigate that fine line between audio branding and noise pollution. However, a key reminder that Greg and many music supervisors echo is that music is chiefly meant to support the consumer experience: discovering the various ways to maximize the power of music and sound for a brand, yet ensuring the sonic identity does not in turn distract from the content or experience.

Thankfully, as disciplines blend and discussions propagate, realizations on the delicacy of music strategy, sonic identity, and audio branding are evolving from farfetched theories into commonly accepted brand assets. Hopefully, the readers of this book continue to innovate the music and sound space that pioneers like Greg Allan have helped shape over the years. Through realizing the full marketing power of music and sound, and their abilities to attract, immerse, and extend consumer experience, readers may revolutionize multiple industries: advertising, television, film, video games, and – most importantly – the music industry.

Spotify Branded Experiences Case Study (Part One)

Imagine a platform where advertising to your target demographic isn't ignored or annoying, and in fact so meaningful that your consumer is inviting a branded experience into the shower with them, on their ride to work, seeking it during lunch, and inviting it to sit at the dinner table with them. That's the role music plays for people, and Spotify has built a platform to allow brands to be part of that experience and lead that conversation throughout the day.

Spotify has been able to excel in brand partnerships because of their vast listening data and the establishment of their brand as a hub for both discovery and relevance for artists and brands. By creating a cohesive branded experience through live activations, Spotify's campaigns set a precedent for effective and mutually beneficial brand partnerships.

One of Spotify's activations, Emerge, a data-driven brand-sponsored franchise, predicts up-and-coming artists with the goal of promoting the sponsoring brand through association with an artist on the rise. The brands that have sponsored Emerge – Globe, Jim Beam, and Ford Fiesta – partnered with Spotify to feature artists in a contest, where the winner was awarded a live concert. Votes are counted through social media shares, following the artists on Spotify, or listening to the artists on Spotify (Spotify, n.d.).

"We always knew our audience, Millennials, to be highly valuable, to be super engaged, and very passionate about not just music, but a host of digital touchpoints and even brands," explained Maureen Traynor, Director of Branded Experiences at Spotify. "We knew that [the value of that audience to brands] was a line in the sand in terms of our positioning to the ad and brand community, and to really defining the value of our audience. The value we can provide to the ad community is a group of people that they're very much trying to reach; but in addition to that audience, it is equally important and incredibly crucial to deliver value to the audience. It's not enough to talk to our constituency. The most effective branded programs on our service also provide some utility or delight" (Traynor, 2015).

According to Maureen, there are a range of ways that Spotify delivers value to its audience. Spotify offers both ad-supported and a premium offering through subscription basis. To support the free offering, Spotify has developed a robust ad program that connects brands with Spotify's audiences through targeted music programs.

"We have an open API, which all sorts of partners can use, including brands, which allows developers to take our catalog, some of our metadata, and some of the music in that catalog, and ship it in ways that are both compelling to a user and that's specific to a brand. So we can, for example, use our API to take suggestions from our audience's favorite songs to sing in the shower and run a campaign with a shampoo brand that actually displays all of those tracks – their favorite songs to sing in the shower – back to the audience," said Maureen.

"We also offer a platform as a place for curation for brands; so, any user, publisher, or artist is able to create profiles on Spotify and then curate any song from our 30 million track catalog into a playlist that they can then use a piece of social content. These activities should be tied back to providing the person they're trying to reach with a piece of content that they're really going to love, and to using music in that way to reach them and identify that piece of content with their brand," said Maureen.

The opportunity Maureen is explaining is a crucial offering for brands. We already know people, specifically Millennials, immerse themselves in music throughout all times and all activities in the day. Spotify has built the platform to allow brands to be involved and supportive of an immersed and continued music experience. Spotify has figured out a method to bring a brand into the shower with you in a non-obtrusive and rewarding way.

As music lovers, we used to look forward to going to the record stores on Tuesdays so we could listen to the new releases and hear what's hot before any of our friends. We'd turn to the radio DJs to hip us to the freshest new bands we should be on the lookout for. But today, with those platforms dissolved, Spotify has built branded experiences that Maureen works with, which strive to create integrated marketing campaigns for more content-driven value, in order to replace these needed music experiences of Spotify's brand partners, Maureen explained. These include Spotify franchises that have been developed in-house, such as the Drop, which celebrates new releases on Spotify with exclusive content as corollary to the music itself (Spotify, n.d.). Another example is Emerge, which is an emerging artist platform that uses streaming data to begin to identify the bands that Spotify predicts will break in the coming months (Spotify, n.d.).

"[In Emerge], we feature in any given cycle ten of those bands that we have identified. We create a friendly competition that takes the streaming data – and also how tracks are being shared and how they're performing on social – and puts them back into a scoring rubric that allows us to narrow the field from ten all the way down to one," said Maureen.

The program has been running for three years and is also live in the Philippines, Canada, Italy, and Spain.

"For both the marketing teams here and the label teams, Emerge is a fantastic way to offer a platform for new artists to get their music out there in a way that's unique to Spotify's platform. It's also been a compelling franchise for brands to support, to get them to be able to infuse the program with their messaging, and to contribute their own support to artists," said Maureen.

According to Maureen, when Spotify partners with a brand to sponsor Emerge, the consumer is always the focus. Providing them with a platform to discover new artists that they might not otherwise find is the true piece of value that consumers seek. When brands get involved, Spotify works with them to create exclusive supplementary content that is tied to a relevant part of the brand's messaging or sonic identity. These might be first-person video content or playlists, all tied back to the same overall theme.

"For example, our current partner on Emerge has a marketing platform that's all about exploration, pushing yourself forward, and getting out and seeing the world. For this partner, we create brand-specific content in the form of interviews and themed playlists," said Maureen. "The point of utility for brands in this specific instance is about creating and distributing artist content that is directly tied to the message they're looking to land with the audience."

As Emerge is integrated with the Spotify platform, engagement analytics can clearly point to the success of the program. Engagement metrics such as streams, page views, time spent with the content and more are standard engagement metrics part of any reporting package, which is largely true industry wide.

"In post-campaign analysis, we start with basic engagement metrics like page views, uniques, time spent, video views, and so on. We add additional analysis around things like week-to-week performance of artists or what specific spikes in listening may be driven [over the course of the program]. For example, artists promoting their participation in a given program is typically a crucial part of how we drive the audience to watch videos, to go to shows, to listen to playlists. We then track the impact that has on engagement in the program. At the outset, we talk about KPIs for our partner and make sure that we were set up to track those in a proper way, and throughout the program we optimize toward those KPIs. That's what's most meaningful to the partner," said Maureen.

Programs such as Emerge not only benefit brands through providing consumers with a comprehensive, discovery-based experience; they also are strong promotional utilities for artists hoping to stand out among the millions of others.

"When you're talking about exploring different avenues for marketing – using new channels that are available today to reach a new audience – artists, labels, and management recognize that brands can be a part of those channels [and] that they have huge social benefits of their own. [When] brands resonate really well with the same kind of age group or demographic that an artist is trying to reach, it really only makes sense to not think solely about the revenue, which is important and shouldn't be discounted, but also to think about using brands' channels to reach a new audience for the band. That's been happening for a long time and isn't new, but it's probably more of a central part of the process around breaking artists than it had been," said Maureen.

"Music, for some brands, might just be a tiny part of their advertising. Some brands are focused only on finding the perfect piece of music to sync to a commercial. But the way fans experience music is actually incredibly broad and robust. People are using music to power all parts of their day, from when they first wake up in the morning to when they get on the train, [...] to what they listen to [...] at work [...] or when they cook dinner, or to get ready to go out, or to unwind to go to sleep. Music is an incredible driver of all of those behaviors and something people connect with every day. That's what we think about at Spotify: how to create products and features that enhance their experience. As a byproduct of doing that we're able to identify and carve out some ways to make that meaningful to our brand partners as well," concluded Maureen.

Maureen and her team are such a powerful example of the burgeoning art of marketing and music. Services like Spotify, Pandora, and

Rdio are no longer simply sites to stream music. By recognizing the marketing power of music, Spotify has created ancillary services like Emerge and Drop that provide brands with an easy way to provide consumers with a valuable experience through music discovery, as well as giving artists a greater platform for exposure and consumers more ways to enjoy music.

Initiatives like these, led by innovators like Maureen, are pushing the boundaries of music and marketing. They're hustling against the grain to resurrect the music industry. Digitization and streaming may have radically altered the landscape of the music industry; however, by leveraging their data in order to create new branded experiences, Maureen and Spotify are helping us all chart a path to sustainability in this revolutionized industry.

Spotify Branded Experiences Case Study (Part Two)

A platform where consumers can engage with and listen to music 24 hours a day is a very meaningful thing in today's world, but as we all know the real meaningful music experience is exactly that – an experience. Nothing will ever replace live music and the rush the concertgoer feels when their heart locks into the beat and they hand over control to the band on stage.

We're far past the days of brands just hanging their logo on stage and thinking that's going to be meaningful or do anything for the consumer. No one remembers who sponsored a show if the only engagement they have with a brand is the logo on the ticket. People need to have their concert experience enhanced by a brand if there's any chance of extending the conversation with the brand after the show ends. Not only has Spotify built a platform to bring music to consumers in more meaningful ways at all hours of the day, but they've also built ways to enhance the live concert experience partnering with brands to foster interaction and engagement with the concertgoer, long before and long after the live event itself.

Sean Haskins has held many different roles throughout his career in the music industry – booking, performing, licensing, and music supervising. Beginning as a drummer for bands in college, Sean spent a lot of time in local venues and eventually apprenticed under a booking agent. From there, he moved to Seattle to apply his booking experience at a local venue. It was initially a means to continue with recording projects and small tours but soon became a full-time career. After that, Sean studied Music Supervision and Licensing, which led him to New York to work on commercials, independent films, and TV pilots. In 2009, Sean found his way back into performing, touring, and working behind the scenes at live events. With a vast array of industry experience and insight, Sean made his way back to New York in 2012, and has since been in charge of the Global Talent Booking & Creative Sync Licensing at Spotify.

"What started out [at Spotify] as primarily a booking role for SXSW, agency gigs, and public-facing events quickly morphed into a licensing role as well," said Sean. "Particularly when it comes to original content. [For example], when we're producing a video of a series of bands that are playing at SXSW. [...] I quickly moved to streamline that process" (Haskins, 2015).

With his experience in so many roles in the music industry, Sean has been crucial to the experiential marketing of Spotify. One of the campaigns that Sean has been involved in at Spotify is their partnership with Blue Moon. Blue Moon's brand has always emphasized the craftsmanship and artistry of their product and created a sense of proper setting for consumers to drink their beer – at festivals, baseball games, or on a summer night with a full moon.

Taking inspiration from their brand identity and story, Spotify partnered with Blue Moon to create the "Follow the Moon" campaign, which was a five-city tour, each of which coincided with a full moon and featured a free concert by different music artists, chef appearances, local artist displays, and Blue Moon beer (Spotify, n.d.). Because of Blue Moon's brand identity and their partnership with Spotify, a service that aims to promote emerging artists, independent artists were ideal for the activations.

"With Blue Moon ... everyone kind of knew what [their] place in the market was. We'd seen their ads before and I knew they'd licensed a Lumineers track for a piece that ran for a little while. [...] I knew where their sensibilities fell as a brand. If you were to equate them to a style of music it would be slightly on the jam side of things, yet melodic and poppy. [...] So that was the first thing that helped us separate who their targets were going to be."

Taking Blue Moon's rated list of bands, Spotify chose the artists Dr. Dog, Typhoon, Moon Taxi, Delta Spirit, and The Temper Trap to headline the activations – artists that fit with the brand identity and who were as enthusiastic about the activations as Spotify and Blue Moon were. To get a brand and artist partnership right, Sean hit on the most important element to achieve success: that of mutual respect and passion for each other's craft and product.

Sean explained that the most successful partnerships between brands and artists feature the brand "[being] as passionate about that band as you would have them be about your brand, and hope that you can have an organic relationship come out of it." The formation of authentic and organic relationships is the ideal for branded events, since they "put a human face on the brand [...] and succeed in identifying with people," said Sean.

Much like Joe Belliotti stated that Coca-Cola's products would always live in the physical world, Blue Moon beer also only exists in the physical world; so, it was important for the brands to create a space for organic artistic expression (a "hodgepodge of culture rather than just four walls with a bar, a stage, and a check," as Sean described), which allowed the artists and consumers to immerse themselves into the activation.

For a successful marketing campaign that includes music, Sean argues that it's more than just finding an artist that fits the brand identity well. The focus on authentic collaboration to achieve both attraction and immersion was the selling point for the artists, the brands, and the consumers.

"Finding a band that isn't necessarily just going to be some sort of spokesperson that's just in it for the money – that's easy – but finding someone who's interested in the way we're trying to communicate these things, like participating in the video, sitting down for an interview with whoever the chef was, or just chatting with commissioned artists that are on-site making Blue Moon-inspired paintings."

Brands look for independent artists because of the mutually beneficial relationship they can bring. Though increased exposure is undeniably a selling point for the artists, as Sean Haskins, said, "You have to come up with actual concrete things to help them rather than saying something vague like 'it's great exposure.' I'm done doing that. I remember throwing that line out when I was trying to get a license on the cheap when I was at my first licensing/music supervision gig. It was when it was all still kind of new. And because I felt like such a schmuck for saying it, I haven't said it since."

Other benefits for the artists in brand partnerships include increased revenue and a potential for future partnerships.

Artists are sensitive to brands tying into their art to promote a product. They want to know they're finding a true partner rather than a one-time meaningless fling. Touring artists get enough of those. Future partnerships between brands and artists can be an extra incentive to artists considering brand partnerships.

"A lot of these bands know that it's not just a one-time opportunity that's on the other end of this, it's a relationship with the brand or even a portfolio of brands, and that might not be a faucet that they necessarily ever want to have turned off. That doesn't mean that they're going to be chasing down sponsorships or branded opportunities all the time, but if they come and have fun and put on a great show and leave a great impression, the brand is going to want to work with them again."

Brand partnerships can be a foot in the door for artists to succeed in the music industry, and besides exposing consumers to new music or providing enhanced live experiences, brand partnerships also benefit the brands that the artists have partnered with.

Obviously partnering with independent artists costs less money than with famous artists does, yet still has the same potential to advance the brand identity as a well-established artist. Another benefit for brands from partnering with independent artists is sustaining relevance by associating their brand identity with artists on the cusp of trends. By focusing on data and analytics of bands he wanted to work with, Sean aimed to maintain the relevance of the Blue Moon brand. Anyone can throw a check at a famous name, but it doesn't extend the relationship with the consumer. Today, brands can use analytics in conjunction with the sonic identity of the band to fortify the relevance of their brand identity and bring unique value and experience to their consumers. Bands that exhibit potential for popularity through listening trends are more attractive in partnerships with brands. Because of Spotify's access to vast amounts of listening data, brands are inclined to work with them to reliably estimate the success for a brand partnership with an independent artist rather than relying on the limited data and personal tastes of their marketing department.

Brands and independent artists mutually benefit from brand partnerships such as the "Follow the Moon" campaign through an exchange of resources – ranging from increased exposure and revenue for the artist to maintaining relevance and saving money for the brand. These partnerships allow each party to achieve their goals while helping the artist avoid the notion of selling out and giving the brand an authentic and relevant brand identity.

More importantly, these type of partnerships and brand experiences give something special to the consumer. The idea of Social Empowerment is focusing on your consumers' passions and enhancing experiences around them. Spotify has built a platform that has been able to achieve this 24 hours a day in the digital world, and brought on the right music and marketing minds to achieve spectacular curated live events in the physical world. With the death of record stores and excitement about new release dates, they've focused on music lovers' needs and brought something meaningful back into our lives.

On top of that, brands no longer have to settle for a banner hanging on the back of a stage as their way of sponsoring a show. Now they have unique ways to truly partner with bands and bring something meaningful to consumers and the music industry itself.

chapter 4 Video Games

Features from Led Zeppelin, original songs by Paul McCartney, playlists curated by DJ Pooh, new releases by A$AP Rocky, private shows by Z-Trip, arena shows by Eminem. With star power that has never come together on one platform before in history, we could only be talking about the video game industry.

Video games have evolved from tacky arcade enclaves for the meek and mild into a multi-sensory experience that spans generations. Couples connect with each other over sweaty games of *Guitar Hero*, fraternities are formed via exclusive guilds of MMO-RPGs, and friendships are tested on the virtual battlefield of online games like *Call of Duty*. What was once considered the domain of basement-dwelling nerds is now the sexiest industry out there, and arguably the fastest growing, too.

Sponsored gamers are earning executive salaries for playing their favorite games, new streaming channels are developed so live matches can be viewed by a global audience, and major brands are tripping over each other as they vie for a chance to get a placement somewhere in the game. The amount of money, technology, and attention that is pouring into the video game industry means, more than anything else, that the gamers demand upgraded experiences regularly – per Social Empowerment. Indie developers are as popular as AAA games, so the best minds in the industry focus their efforts on creating a better gaming world in order to satisfy the passion points of their consumers lest they lose them to a competitor's open-world saga. Games of all kinds have a higher expectation of believability, immersion, and experience – the gameworld, however fictitious and fantastical, must be experienced as its own complete world.

And just as in our physical world, music must therefore play a significant role in order to deliver on that promise of premier experience.

Although games can form cult-like followings and entice diehard fans to wait in line overnight for new releases, the gaming industry undoubtedly knows there is still a massive audience and demographics they have yet to attract and convert into obsessive gamers. In addition to innovating game styles and plotlines that could never have been conceived in the pre-gen era of DreamCast and the original NES, the game industry is also pioneering in its marketing techniques to attract the previously marginalized demographics of women, consumers over the age of 30, and more. Such is the marketing power of the gaming industry's innovation that more people will probably consider it more socially engaging to quit the co-ed volleyball team and instead join an after-dinner Halo LAN party.

Part of that marketing muscle – as well as the game and story development – is music.

In fact, some of the most forward-thinking minds in music supervision have been concentrating on identifying strategy for music immersion along every path in a video gamer's world. Audio fidelity has evolved in such a way that there are nearly boundless opportunities to integrate music as seamlessly into a video game as they would any other audiovisual experience, if not more so. Layering the music through audio stems so that it reacts to character movement and player decisions; hunting for the hottest new artists and becoming a trusted platform to break new songs; leveraging the power of reach to help artists break and cross-promote with other brands – all this and more has magnified the buzz around games, gamers, and gaming events into an infectious siren of possibility. Video game music supervisors must juggle more factors than simply what's the best song to complement the visuals on-screen; however, one silver lining in their complex list of duties is the fact that artists – emerging and established, unknown and famous – will do anything these days to get their music played in a video game.

In fact, artists now look to gamers as peers of cultural relevance – many top rankers on *RuneScape* or *World of Warcraft*, for example, have racked up more Twitter followers for their virtual prominence than some artists can do over years of touring. Gamers are selling out arenas and play in front of millions of people, raking in millions of dollars. Gamers reach more people as individuals playing out of their mom's house than a famous musician does with a full major label promotional budget and professional marketing team behind them. In many respects, gamers have become the rock stars for a very niche, yet inclusive, demographic of consumers. And the video game industry knows it.

The most epic use of music and immersive entertainment in media today belongs to video games. As the fastest growing area of the media industry, they're not just throwing parties like rock stars; they represent everything about being a rock star. The best live promotional activations, the biggest parties with exclusive performances by top talent, even the most sophisticated orchestral performances – all are the byproduct of the video game industry. From being able to break new music by emerging artists as well as to call on the most famous acts in history to license songs or create new music, the video game industry is the current and the future of opportunity for the music industry.

Paul McCartney, Led Zeppelin, Jay Z, Eminem, the world's best orchestras, and the coolest new bands all share at least one thing in common – they will do anything to be part of a video game. But regardless of the name, the music supervisors still follow the same rules of music strategy – attraction, immersion, and extension – in order to achieve success through music.

Video game music supervisors must consider how to attract new consumers to the game, how to immerse them into the game world, and how to extend the relationship between the consumer and the game even after the final boss battle.

My company Music Dealers reviewed the ten top games of recent years in our 2015 article, "1UP or KO'd: A Music Agency's Review of Music in Today's Video Games" (Miller, *1UP or KO'd: A Music Agency's Review of Music in Today's Video Games*, 2015). Here's what we discovered.

"Games are better understood as platforms for experiences than as products," wrote Dr. Hanna Wirman in the article, "Fan Productivity and Fandom" (Wirman, 2009). If that is true, then what is the role of music in those platforms for experiences?

As is the case for many mediums, the role of music is multifaceted. Music can lure consumers to video games through advertisements and promotions. Music can further immerse gamers into that platform and enhance their experience. Music can even maintain the players' experience beyond the gameplay, extending the relationship between the game and the consumer into other mediums like live concerts and soundtracks.

Music is one of the key components that can elevate a video game from simply a product to truly a platform for experience. Theoretically, music is also one of the easiest components of a video game to leverage. Advanced sound design in games allows for creative ways to use music, such as adaptive music and layered stems.

Additionally, the music industry is virtually flooded with artists willing and eager to collaborate with video game developers, studios, and publishers on marketing campaigns and in-game syncs.

Theory, however, is seldom universally applied in reality. For that reason, we wanted to take a look at the industry and analyze how far developers, studios, and publishers are pushing the use of music in and around their video game titles.

Is music really helping transform video games from simple products into platforms for experiences?

It's easy to play a game through once and say, "Yes, I love the music!" or "What the hell was the composer thinking?" Just check the message boards: these conversations happen all the time.

We wanted to create a system that could objectively measure how music functions in today's video games. It's more of a questionnaire, really: nine "yes or no (or maybe)" questions about how music is applied to a video game, including before its launch, in the gameplay, and after its release. We decided that a "yes" would earn one point for the game, a "maybe" would earn a half-point for the game, and a "no" would just not count at all.

We split the overall score of a game into three categories: "1Up" if the game earned six points or higher, "AFK (Away From Keyboard)" if it earned between three to six points; and "KO'd" if it earned less than three points.

After playing through the games, researching their development, and answering the questionnaire, we found the average score for the games by simply adding them up and dividing the sum by the number of games we studied. We figured that by studying the ten top-selling games of the past three years – two from 2013, five from 2014, and three from 2015 – we would be able to determine a fair analysis of the state of the industry of music in video games.

A Review of Today's Video Games

Here are the nine questions we asked ourselves after playing through and researching the development of each game:

1. Does the game have a clear and consistent "sound" (i.e., "sonic identity")?
2. Does the game use music creatively to promote before its release?
3. Does the music of the game's promotion align with its overall "sound" or "sonic identity"?
4. Does the in-game music immerse players into the gameplay?
5. Does the in-game music integrate with the story of the game?
6. Does the licensed music and the score blend to immerse players into the gamespace?
7. Did the developers, studio, or publisher use music after the game's release to continue engagement with gamers?
8. If so, do these new touchpoints align with the game's overall "sound" or "sonic identity"?
9. Did the developers, studio, or publisher partner with artists to cross-promote the game and music?

Here are our comments on the top-selling games.

Grand Theft Auto V (2013): 8.5 out of 9 … 1Up!

The Grand Theft Auto franchise has always been noted for its use of licensed music in its gameplay, and the highly anticipated *Grand Theft Auto V* pushed that trend even further than previous titles. Ivan Pavlovich, music supervisor at Rockstar Games, created a West Coast soundscape that appropriately fit the Los Angeles-inspired setting of the game's Los Santos gamespace. The game also features tons of licensed tracks for the franchise's acclaimed radio stations, many of which were original songs, such as Tyler the Creator's track, "Garbage." Additionally, the stations were DJ'd by real-life artists of note, like the

West Coast Classics station hosted by DJ Pooh. Furthermore, *GTA V* was the first of the series to include an original score, which Pavlovich was careful to use to support – not replace – the licensed music that has become a staple of the franchise. While Spotify playlists, downloadable music, and purchasable soundtracks were released, [we still feel] they could've done more with music in the game's marketing strategy.

Call of Duty: Ghosts (2013): 6.5 out of 9 … 1Up!

In an interview with *Billboard*, Activision's CMO Tim Ellis states that the publisher's research has indicated that fans of Call of Duty are also big fans of Eminem, which led to a comprehensive partnership between the rapper and *Call of Duty: Ghosts*. Eminem released his song "Survival" in the game's official trailer, and also created his own music video for the song with content inspired by the game. "Survival" was also featured in the game itself and in its end credits. GameStop, Activision, and Eminem also released copies of *Call of Duty: Ghosts* with a download code for Eminem's album, *The Marshall Mathers LP 2*, and an exclusive song. Both the game and the album debuted on the same day to increase cross-promotional impact. While David Buckley's original soundtrack for the game supports the story of *Ghosts*, we think the franchise will entail even more immersive music in its future titles.

Destiny (2014): 5.5 out of 9 … AFK!

Maintaining the esteemed lineage of the Halo series, Bungie launched its newest franchise *Destiny* in 2014 with celebrated composer Martin O'Donnell at the helm of its music strategy, along with his professional partner, Michael Salvatori. O'Donnell, renowned for his work throughout the Halo series, collaborated with Paul McCartney to create the sound of *Destiny*. O'Donnell and his team crafted a strong sonic identity of the game through its orchestral score; however, the music of the game's marketing strategy could be seen as inconsistent. Additionally, *Destiny* didn't seem to use music beyond releasing the soundtrack for purchase and working with Paul McCartney on an arguably awkward music video.

Madden NFL 15 (2014): 2.5 out of 9 … KO'd!

EA Sports is a titan of licensed music, having worked with numerous artists over the past decade to debut singles and feature original music. However, *Madden NFL 15* did not seem to live up to the standards of its predecessors. Since 2013, the Madden games have employed an orchestral soundtrack to score the game, simulating the sounds of the NFL when it airs on television networks like CBS. While the game's score, written by composer Mark Petrie, accurately fit the sonic identity of the NFL, fans of the franchise have expressed a hope for more licensed music, as featured in previous titles. Thankfully, EA Trax, a platform that has been recognized as the industry's foremost showcase for introducing new music, is returning to the series in *Madden NFL 16*. Accordingly, we expect this next installment of the series to earn plenty of 1Ups for its creative use of music.

Watch Dogs (2014): 6 out of 9 … 1Up!

After receiving over 80 awards and nominations for its display at E3 2012, *Watch Dogs* was one of the hottest games of 2014 and employed music in a variety of ways. Composer Brian Reitzell carefully shaped the soundtrack by blending sounds of Chicago, the setting of the game, with synthesized layers of organic instruments in order to fit the futuristic plot of the game. Additionally, *Watch Dogs* features tons of licensed music, as well as an in-game app called "Song Sneak" that operates like Shazam, in which the player can identify songs playing in stores or vehicles, download them onto the character's phone, and afterwards stream them during gameplay. The in-game use of music in *Watch Dogs* was very comprehensive, though its use outside of the game – in its promotions, trailers, and marketing campaigns – was sometimes inconsistent and didn't seem to fully capture the power of music as a means of engagement.

Super Smash Bros. for Nintendo 3DS and Wii U (2014):
7.5 out of 9 … 1Up!

Nintendo has always used music uniquely, and the original music by composer Koji Kondo has developed a devoted following ever since the original *Super Mario Bros.* The cultural reverence of his music continued with the release of *Super Smash Bros. for Nintendo 3DS and Wii U*, which included groundbreaking features like allowing players to customize in-game playlists and listen to the soundtrack while the 3DS is in "sleep mode." The official soundtrack, "A Smashing Soundtrack," is a two-disc product of 72 music tracks total and was shipped to eligible Club Nintendo members after the game's release. Also, the Nintendo created a music page on the game's official website that lists some of the original tracks.

Titanfall (2014) 6 out of 9 … 1Up!

Created by some of the key developers behind the Call of Duty franchise, *Titanfall* earned over 60 awards at its E3 2013 reveal. Composer Stephen Barton created the original soundtrack to the game and crafted separate sonic identities for the two opposing *Titanfall* teams to further immerse players into the war-torn colonies of the game's setting. The score successfully blends into the gameplay; however, few touchpoints were leveraged beyond releasing the soundtrack on Spotify, iTunes, and other sites. Run DMT's remix of "Revolution" by Diplo was synced in one commercial, which accurately fit the theme of the game. The artist promoted the placement on his SoundCloud account; otherwise, music didn't seem to be a key component in the marketing strategy of the game.

The Legend of Zelda: Majora's Mask 3D (2015):
6 out of 9 … 1Up!

Nintendo recently recreated its iconic title, *The Legend of Zelda: Majora's Mask*, for its 3DS platform. The game itself incorporates music immensely into the plot and gameplay, as players learn and perform songs on various instruments in order to navigate the story. Additionally, the live orchestra The Legend of Zelda: Symphony of the Goddesses features music from the game in its new "Master Quest" tour. The Nintendo 3DS eShop also synced a song from the game, "Song of Storms," to play for a limited time to promote *Majora*'s release. Consistent with most Nintendo titles, however, the publisher didn't collaborate with artists on cross-promotional opportunities.

Bloodborne (2015): 4.5 out of 9 … AFK!

Critically acclaimed following its March 2015 release, *Bloodborne* features a powerful soundtrack composed by Yuka Kitamura, Tsukasa Saitoh, Nobuyoshi Suzuki, Ryan Amon, and Michael Wandmacher. The score captures the dark atmosphere of the game's Dracula-inspired setting and was recently released for purchase. Beyond the score, the game did not seem to fully leverage music in its promotion, development, or marketing. For example, "Hunt You Down" by production company The Hit House was synced to the game's official trailer and received significant consumer interest. The company released a full version of the song on its SoundCloud page, but the publisher has yet to maximize the marketing power of the song.

Mortal Kombat X (2015): 3.5 out of 9 … KO'd!

Released in April 2015 as the tenth main installment to the Mortal Kombat series, *Mortal Kombat X* continues the franchise with composer Dan Forden as its audio director. To promote the release of the game, the marketing team behind *Mortal Kombat X* teamed up with a couple different artists in very impressive ways. For example, rapper

Wiz Khalifa created an original song for the game, "Can't Be Stopped," which was featured in the debut trailer and opening cinematic of *Mortal Kombat X*. Additionally, the team collaborated with the bassist of the rock band System of a Down to direct the official television commercial and launch the trailer for the game, which also featured the band's 2001 hit song, "Chop Suey!," though to mixed reviews. Beyond those key uses, music doesn't seem to be a highlight in the marketing campaign of the game; however, because the game's release is still fairly recent, the publisher may incorporate music to greater effect.

All in all, the state of the industry of music in video games seems to be growing. The average score of these ten games is 5.65, teetering between AFK and 1Up status.

Music Strategy and the Ten Core Audio Touchpoints

While reviewing these games, we realized how creatively music supervisors, audio directors, composers, and publishers are applying music strategy into their work. Never before has music been considered with such care in the promotion, development, and marketing of a video game, as is evident in the innovations of these ten titles.

The game music of today's industry is leaps and bounds ahead of the music strategy of earlier gaming generations. Music supervision and sound design have become venerated components of the video game industry; therefore, we expect studios, developers, and publishers to look to music as a tool of attraction, immersion, and extension even more in 2016.

In order for video games to truly become platforms of experiences rather than simply products, music must become integral components of each step of a video game's lifespan. Isn't that the case in life, the original platform of experiences? (Miller, *1UP or KO'd: A Music Agency's Review of Music in Today's Video Games*, 2015).

Nice to note, even the game with the lowest score leveraged music far more creatively than its predecessors of even ten years ago. The rise of the video game music supervisor has ascended in tandem with the evolution of audio technology in games, the cultural value of music, and the Social Empowerment of gamers. All of these have collided to result in these ten core audio touchpoints of the video game industry:

1. Sonic Identity: The interactivity of video games allows for a wide array of ways to establish a game's sonic identity. Consider for example the distinct, yet very different, sonic identities of both Tetris and the Halo franchise.
2. Promo Commercials: Often handled by a different department, music in promotional commercials is a powerful way to attract consumers to the game. As explained in the section that immediately follows, last year we reviewed five games of E3 that premiered with incredible music experiences in their promos.
3. Non-diegetic Sync: Used often in the film and television worlds, this is music that the character perceivably does not hear, but the player does.
4. Diegetic Sync: On the other hand, this is music that happens in the gameplay, sometimes called source.
5. In-Game Music Experience: This is the interactive phenomenon in which the player uses music in the game in order to affect the gameplay and gameworld.
6. Social Media: As in other industries, games can turn to social media as a way of extending relationships beyond the screen, and can use music as a passion point to do so.
7. Web Page: Developers like Rock Star and more have web pages where all things music are collected for gamers to experience outside of the game.
8. Artist Relationships: Curated playlists by big-name DJs or commissioning custom music for a game, artist relationships are powerful ways to attract consumers to the game.

9. Asset Monetization: Soundtracks, vinyl, and more are all ways for a game to enter the music industry and monetize their music as a product in and of itself.
10. Live Activation: Game music has totally changed the orchestra scene, and music has become an integral part of any video game event.

We've tracked down the best minds across the video game industry to learn how they are creating repeatable processes for successful music supervision, as well as artists who have directly benefited from partnering with games. Following are some case studies that have resulted from our research.

Top 5 Most Musically Engaging Games of E3

Electronic Entertainment Expo, commonly known as E3, is the premier annual trade fair for the video game industry, used by video game publishers and developers to reveal and advertise their upcoming games through gameplay demos, promotional commercials, and onsite activations. Numerous industry pundits have reviewed these premieres, but few have explored how music is leveraged by publishers and developers to engage with fans during their games' big reveal.

So, we took a look and determined the Top Five Most Musically Engaging Games of E3. Game on.

1. *Adr1ft* | 505 Games

   Set in the dark, silent void of space, *Adr1ft* by 505 Games used music in a way few astral media have done before. According to an IGN interview with the developers, the game was inspired in part by the music of Pink Floyd, and the rock band Weezer reportedly contributed to the soundtrack, too. Additionally, the trailer for the game features Beethoven's "Moonlight Sonata," though listeners will most likely recognize the tune as the iconic melody to Metallica's "Nothing Else Matters." The haunting song is what makes this space-based ad especially stellar.

2. *Guitar Hero Live* | Activision
   The general gameplay behind *Guitar Hero Live* will be familiar to most gamers – pretending to play a guitar to match visual cues on the screen. However, there have been numerous updates to the franchise since the last *Guitar Hero* to evolve the music game into an even greater rock band experience. Synced to an interactive, full-motion video, gameplay simulates a real-world concert setting from the first-person perspective of the guitarist. The game's soundtrack will include songs by The Black Keys, Ed Sheeran, Of Mice and Men, and more, as well as tons of downloadable content to keep gamers' set-lists rockin'.
3. *Battleborn* | 2K Games
   Developed by the same creators of popular game *Borderlands*, *Battleborn* is a first-person shooter with a large focus on its online multiplayer arena elements. To advertise this feature, its E3 2015 trailer, "Battleborn: For Every Kind of Badass," portrays the 25 different characters you can play as. The ad opens with the popular dub-pop song, "Fitzpleasure," by English indie rockers alt-J. Formed in 2008, the band has experienced recent worldwide acclaim and appeared at Chicago's 2015 Lollapalooza festival at the end of July, only weeks after 2K Games premiered "Battleborn: For Every Kind of Badass." At the time of writing the ad had been viewed 4.8 million times since its June 4 release.
4. *EA Sports 16 Lineup* | EA Games
   As the music team at EA Games continues to demonstrate, music plays a big role in its sports titles; the premieres of *FIFA 16*, *Madden NFL 16*, *NBA Live 16*, and *NHL 16* proved that is still the case. EA revealed that EA Trax, the title of the in-game soundtracks on their video games, would be reintegrated into

Madden NFL 16 and that the publisher will also partner with Spotify to bring back the most popular songs from previous titles of the Madden franchise. Additionally, NBA Live 16's "Official E3 First Look Trailer" features "Out the Trunk out the Trunk" from hip-hop artist Fashawn's second studio album, *The Ecology*, which was released in February 2015.

5. *Assassin's Creed Syndicate* | Ubisoft
   The newest addition to the critically acclaimed Assassin's Creed franchise, *Syndicate* is set in London amid the Industrial Revolution as players navigate the city's corridors of organized crime during the Victorian era. To maximize the effect of its highly anticipated trailer, Ubisoft synced "In The Heat of the Moment" by Noel Gallagher's High Flying Birds, the solo moniker of former Oasis lead guitarist Noel Gallagher. The band promoted the sync on its site, and at the time of writing the YouTube video had been viewed 5.9 million times since its June 15 release.

As demonstrated, the music of the promotional videos and releases was a pivotal component of the games' presentation and appeal to consumers. Out of the hundred or so games that premiered at the event, these five stood out to us and to many other video game analysts as the games to watch – and what first attracted us to them was their strategic use of music to attract eyes and ears to their content.

EA Sports Case Study

The use of music in video games is not a new field. Personally, although I was never a big video game player, I couldn't wait for the new *Tony Hawk* games to be released. It was the number one way I discovered cool new artists, and I'll never forget the first time I heard Del the Funky Homosapien while my friends sat around in our dorm room playing. Video games have always been a great resource to discover new music; however, the past decade has improved the industry of game music by leaps and bounds. At the helm of this journey to a new sonic frontier has been EA Games, the publisher behind franchises such as Need for Speed and FIFA. In 2001, music executive Steve Schnur joined EA to lead its music endeavors and spearheads the creative vision for all EA global releases and franchises as the Worldwide Executive and President of EA Music Group (Kawashima).

Video games have always been a great resource to discover new music

Though by 2001 Schnur had already served in executive positions at music monoliths such as BMG and EMI, some were surprised at his arrival to EA Games. The video game industry had simply yet to capitalize on the power of music. Similarly, the music industry had yet to fully realize the potential of video games as a vehicle for music promotion and collaboration.

"I had heard EA had brought in this in-house music guy to do, at that point I wasn't sure what," remembered Raphaella (Raphi) Lima in a phone interview. "Was he going to open up a label? What is this guy doing?" (Lima, 2015).

In 2001, Raphi was working with Tim Riley at Go Big! Entertainment Inc. on music programming and licensing in action sports movies, feature films, and video games, including *Tony Hawk's Gigantic Skate Park Tour*, *Travis Pastrana: Revelation 199*, and more. Riley, the current SVP Artist & Label Relations at TIDAL, founded Go Big! and recruited Raphi while she was producing the first music magazine on DVD format, called 750MPH. Despite her complete immersion in the space, it wasn't long before then that Raphi discovered the depth of the music industry.

"I just thought to get into that world you had to be a musician," Raphi said. "I never really thought about the music business, I wasn't

exposed to that [in Brazil]. And once I got to LA during my senior year of school, I started learning, wow, there is a world here when it comes to music, and there's so many different roles that you can play within that beyond just creating music, which was very exciting."

According to Raphi, shortly after hearing of Steve's arrival to EA games, her long-time friend and collaborator, Cybele Pettus, went to meet Steve and returned with a job.

"I was like, 'What? Oh no, I've got to work with you, too,'" Raphi said. "So a month later, they had some paid internship position. I didn't care what it was, I just needed my foot in the door. I was obsessed with EA, it was definitely a dream come true, and I didn't care what it was. I was just like, 'Get me in there!' So we came in. Cybele was Steve's first hire, I was the second hire, and it's been the three of us for thirteen years doing what we do when it comes to music here at EA."

"I started as his assistant, but I was already doing [music supervision] prior to being here," Raphi continued. "I remember one day the guys were wrapping up *FIFA 2003* at the time I started, and I was looking at the list. It was all British bands, and I was like, 'Man, this is these people's idea of soccer and football music. This is crazy!' So I made a little mixtape and I brought it in. I had music from Brazil, Japan, Colombia, and I was like, 'This is what football sounds like around the world. This is the sound of football.'"

According to Raphi, some of the bands on her playlist ended up breaking into mainstream success several months later, including a Brazilian artist whose music was placed in a movie from the United States. This validated her skills in music supervision to Steve, Raphi said, and she earned her chance at supervising her first game the year after, *FIFA 2004*.

"Music is very subjective," Raphi said. "Everybody's an expert, everybody has an opinion about it, but at the end of the day I think music supervisors in particular succeed at being able to add to the mood or the storytelling of the piece they're working with, but to also really be able to identify and call out trends very, very early on."

As in films and in some ad campaigns, production times in games can extend for months or even years. Therefore, music supervisors for video games have the additional struggle in which they must not only discover music that appropriately suits the content and story of the game, but they must also be able to anticipate the music trends that will hit once the game actually is launched on the market. The soundtrack to *FIFA 2004* featured a diverse selection of 40 songs from a range of artists, including Japanese rock group Babamania and Danish indie rock duo The Raveonettes. *FIFA 2004* also featured the song, "Rhythm Bandits," by Danish pop musical duo Junior Senior, which charted in the UK and Australia. "Nothing But You" also made the list, which was performed by German EDM DJ Paul van Dyk, who was the first artist to receive a Grammy nomination in the category of Best Dance/Electronic album in 2004.

"It's not just, 'Hey, I like music and this is good music,'" Raphi said. "There's a lot of different variables that come into it, and you have to be in tune with culture and in tune with trends, really be aware of what's coming and what's going, and sense where things are going to be at these points in time when your project or production is going to go out and it's going to connect with what's happening and what's relevant then. It has to be timeless, in that sense."

At the inception of EA's dream team of music execs, Raphi said Steve spent a great amount of time traveling the world, sitting down with labels and publishers to educate them on the wealth of opportunity that video games offered the music industry.

"I think that when Steve started this, he had an incredible vision to look at the gaming space and gamers, and the amount of time that these kids were putting into this experience," Raphi said. "And how much of a missed opportunity he was seeing in regards to putting new music in front of this really captive audience. [...] It could be a great vehicle to expose new music to a new audience."

"We used to go and educate the music industry on what we can do for them," Raphi continued. "Now, every major label, indies, publishers, artist management, and everybody in between comes to us early on, and we're a part of that marketing plan and we're a part of the launch plan. We've become really ingrained as one of those tools for an artist to get into a certain market and roll out new music and break into new audiences."

Every video game naturally caters to a certain demographic, an audience that can grow or narrow depending on its marketing campaigns, including by using music as a marketing tool. For example, as soccer (or football) is allegedly the most popular sport in the world, it naturally caters to an international audience. Therefore, it can function as a powerful vehicle for pushing an artist's music out to a global community. On the other hand, an artist might share a key target audience with a game like *Battlefield: Hardline*, which would make a partnership between the two entities a powerful collaboration, with extensive opportunities for cross-promotional marketing.

For example, in 2013 Drake developed an endorsement with EA Sports and FIFA, after which he appeared across ESPN to discuss his love for both the international sport and the video game. Additionally, EA Sports enlisted Drake to announce the upcoming release of *FIFA 14* during E3 2013 and featured the rapper in a TV commercial, "We Are FIFA 14." Drake also headed the game's launch party at New York City's Union Square Ballroom, where he challenged Australian football professional Tim Cahill in a filmed match on *FIFA 14*. Furthermore, consumers saved $5 on Drake's *Nothing Was the Same* album when purchasing with *FIFA 14*, both of which were released on the same day.

"I was trying to get *FIFA* some notoriety in the North American market, while Drake still had markets to break into internationally," Raphi said of the endorsement. "It was a great partnership that we had, where he definitely benefitted me in my penetration here in the North American space, and they were able to open up the doors in some territories where he just really didn't have a presence."

The year before, for its *FIFA 13* title, EA Sports also strove to increase its relevance in North American markets, according to Raphi. She said that it was the game's first big attempt to break into the U.S., and she had a three-second opportunity to get somebody's face on the screen for the game's TV adverts that young people in the U.S. would recognize and relate to.

"I'm like, 'OK, there's very few people in the world who, after seeing their face in a couple seconds, they're going to know who they are.' And that's how we ended up going with Snoop," Raphi said. "But I said [...], 'There's also this new kid coming up who's a big fan of *FIFA* and I think that we could get a lot out of being associated with someone really early on and who is a fan of the game. I think you guys should take a look at A$AP Rocky as well.'"

EA Sports released the spots online and aired them on television. At least three ads were created – "Join the Club" and two "Better With Kinect" spots. Snoop Dogg was featured in all three and A$AP Rocky appeared in one of them. According to Raphi, social media conversations around the brand skyrocketed after the ads hit. Most interesting to her, though, was the fact that the hottest topic of discussion was split down the middle between Snoop and A$AP – rap's most well-known figurehead and an up-and-coming star. According to Raphi, knowing the emerging artists whose growth young people are watching is an important component of modern music supervision, especially for a game like *FIFA*.

"I definitely pay attention to that now that I'm more in the marketing side of things," said Raphi. "If these guys are shooting the next

Need For Speed commercial or something for *Star Wars*, I'm going to look at who their audience is and what's happening there, and figure out how I can tell that story and connect them with an artist, a song, or something in the music space that is very specific to their target demographic."

While supervising the music for TV and web commercials and the music for in-game use may seem to employ similar skillsets, Raphi said the process is completely different. It's worth noting that supervisors across television and film industries have expressed similar opinions. In fact, the music for commercials and advertising campaigns is often handled from an entirely separate team than the music for in-game, TV, or film.

"When it comes to the in-game music, the supervisor will have so much control, so you're able to keep so much more of that creative integrity in there. You work with a point person or two on the development side of things and it's very connected. The focus there is to really come up with, depending on the title you're working with, a soundtrack that's going to build the story that you want to tell, or trigger the emotions that you're trying to get across. I think from the creative standpoint it's a much more rewarding process in a way, just because there's so much more of you that I feel goes into the final product."

"When you're working with marketing and advertising, there's just so many variables," Raphi continued. "These past three years, since I've moved from being an in-game music supervisor and now really focus on global music partnerships and music marketing opportunities, I try to find out how I can influence what the agencies are feeling and how that correlates back to what we're doing with the actual in-game music."

This integration of the project's in-game music strategy with its marketing initiatives is a factor that many productions – in video games, television shows, films, and more – do not employ with enough effect. Converging the marketing touchpoints with the game through a consistent music strategy strengthens the sonic efficacy of each element, from the commercials to the cut-scenes.

A common struggle for many music supervisors is finding a balance between doing what's best for the marketing of the product and doing what's best for experiencing the content. Partnering with one artist for the game's sponsorship might yield astounding reach that the game would never have otherwise accessed; however, it might not communicate the true character of the game's story in the way that other music might. Conversely, syncing a song for an in-game cinematic might perfectly capture the emotional essence of the game and pull at players' heartstrings more powerfully than anything, but it might offer little to no marketing potential for the game overall.

This struggle between creativity and marketability begs the question, is there a way to get the best of both worlds? Can one maximize the reach and power of music, but also support the content with the music that it absolutely needs?

"I think in order for you to be successful, the music needs to fit and needs to be good in the first place," said Raphi. "I do not believe in putting something in there just because the artist is big or because there's a big reach or if the reasons are not taken into consideration what the piece really needs to elevate it and bring it to the next level. So I'm a believer that the music needs to come first; but, if you're working on a spot that is going to be global and you're trying to get through to a certain audience or communicate a specific message, then you need to take those variables into consideration to find a song that delivers across all of it."

"So you need to address the integrity of the product, and find the music that is going to deliver that next level for you," said Raphi. "But you are looking to find something that will ultimately fit those marketing needs, i.e., something that's going to spread socially or generate viral views."

This duality of music supervision that Raphi experiences every day at EA will eventually become the norm for all video games and types of content, including television, film, and even branded content. The marketing power of music in video games is multifaceted and profound, and music is leveraged across a wide array of touchpoints – from promoting the release of a game in TV ads and web campaigns, to integrating authentic music into its storyline and partnering with real musicians during development, to continuing to engage consumers after they've completed the game through ancillary touchpoints like live concerts or Spotify playlists. All of these, in one way or another, contribute to the marketing of the video game; as such, more supervisors should be looking at the cross-functionality of video game music as Raphi does.

Her role as head of Global Music Partnerships and Marketing focuses exactly on that point; however, as Raphi expressed, it is still a relatively new position, and one which reportedly arose organically from the results of the music efforts of EA's music team.

"As we evolved here and we started to get feedback from artists and partners directly, as to the impact that those placements were having in those artists' career," said Raphi, "we started to realize that we just weren't having the time to connect the dots from when you were placing the tracks in the game to when you were having to move on and program the next game. Also when we started here, we were doing sixty titles a year, whether that was original songs or licensing, and it was just a lot of work. So, over the years, EA has focused on bigger and better titles, and we're no longer working on sixty titles a year. Maybe we're working on fifteen or twenty titles that really need to have that music focus and a deeper integration."

According to EA's site, the publisher released around ten games in 2014, including those for mobile operating systems. EA released

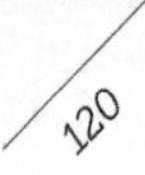

around 20 in 2013 and around 30 in 2012, once again including those for mobile operating systems. Several years ago, EA released around 60 titles in both 2009 and 2005. The year Raphi started at EA, 2002, the publisher released about 45 titles (EA Games, n.d.).

"So, with that, I think we really saw an opportunity to look at having one person dedicated to bringing the music in-game, and then having another person to look at what is happening in-game to build on that and go beyond the placements. You can now partner with the artists to deliver on marketing strategies, retail needs, and fulfill various initiatives that can benefit from music. So, it just really made a lot of sense and it's been good."

One such project that EA released and that Raphi worked on was the popular *2014 FIFA World Cup* game, the official video game for the 2014 FIFA World Cup championship. A prominent part of the game's appeal was its soundtrack, which features 34 tracks by artists from all over the world, including Israel, Mexico, the United States, and of course the host country, Brazil. Two Music Dealers artists, Felix Weber and Holger, joined the coveted lineup of worldwide musicians. Authenticity and diversity were essential requisites for the music, according to Brandon Smith, Vice President (US West) of Music Dealers, who coordinated with the creative teams on the FIFA project. By joining the iconic soundtrack of *2014 FIFA World Cup*, the artists' music streamed through consoles across the globe (Music Dealers, n.d.).

In many cases, successful music strategies in media like video games or television are a happy accident that resulted from the supervisors' simple desire to sync good, authentic music into their projects. Because of Steve's foresight on the convergence of the video games and music industries in the early 2000s, this was not completely the case. Music was chosen very deliberately since the onset. However, one might speculate that the marketing power of music for EA's titles was stronger than its actual employment in the marketing strategy warranted. In other words, the music – especially of EA Sports titles like *Madden* and *FIFA* – did much more than anyone anticipated, especially as it was hardly leveraged in the marketing strategy of these titles at the turn of the century.

This realization fostered the development of Raphi's new role, which she seems to be filling with appropriate creativity, if her most recent push with *Madden* is any indication.

Since 2012, the music of *Madden* has been scored largely by an orchestral soundtrack, one which seemed to fit the sonic identity of the NFL franchise and the sound of televised games; however, this music strategy clearly digressed from previous titles, in which licensed music was placed to great effect. According to Raphi, not only is this strategy returning for *Madden NFL 16*, but EA is also pushing music even further in the game's promotion to attract new players and some they might have lost along the way.

"[We're] bringing music back to *Madden* in the way that we used to do three years ago," said Raphi, "and have an opportunity to partner with Live Nation to [give] $15 of Concert Cash if you [pre-order] *Madden* at GameStop, and now we have the Spotify profile and we're going to feature 23 weeks of programming during the football season with new music as they hit the market, themed lists and team/athlete-inspired updates. This way we can also push out new music to *Madden* audiences that we really didn't have a chance to cover in-game."

"So, [working in global music partnerships and marketing] just really allows us to create more," Raphi continued. "At first, I would finish *FIFA* and I would move on to programming the next title; I couldn't think about what I could do with those artists post launch. Now I can go in and do content with these guys. [...] It really allowed us to be more thorough with the work that we were doing and, in a way, now provide the music industry with even more opportunities with how we use music here."

Because of the highly interactive nature of games, the music industry is looking to video games more and more as a vehicle for promotion and expansion. There are so many ways to collaborate with developers and studios, whether for in-game or commercial use. But artists aren't the only ones to benefit from this partnership; as Raphi explained regarding the Drake sponsorship for *FIFA*, it allowed the franchise greater access into the North American market. And in the previous year, for *FIFA 2013*, the game reportedly sold 4.5 million copies worldwide in five days, to become the biggest sports video game launch of all time (Nichols, 2012).

Despite success stories such as these, music departments in all industries struggle to prove the correlation between a strong music strategy and product sales. Music supervision is a craft of nuance and art; therefore, it can be difficult to pinpoint direct sales figures whose spikes or surges were directly affected by the music. This is especially true because music is only one of many factors that go into any production.

"I had to get quite creative over the last few years because that transition happened as a whole within the company, where metrics and results and measurements and whatnot were very much the main topic, and I definitely found myself looking at ways to attach R.O.I. to creative," Raphi said. "I look at what their success metrics are, what their KPIs are, and I then look at how I'm going to connect my efforts to the results that they can measure."

"So, you come up with different strategies that can speak to what they look at as successful in order to sell your fish, as they say in Brazil," said Raphi.

"I think that music allows you to have a personal connection with the consumers that you will not always get through other marketing avenues," said Raphi. "In that way, you are enhancing that entertainment experience, while you are also using music to further your relevance

in that cultural space. [...] You really use music in that sense to create the identity [of a video game], and you're also using music to then get to a consumer that you might not have yet, and you know that music is the way to get to their heart."

JDP Artist Success Story

JDP isn't a huge gamer, but he made sure to play *Watch Dogs* when his little cousin bought a copy of the game after its summer 2014 debut. JDP sat and played through a good portion of the game, hacking his way through the underground crime ring of the fictitious Chicago setting, discovering songs via the in-game phone app, "Song Sneak." Eventually, after eavesdropping on enough non-playable characters (NPCs) and frequenting a few virtual pawn shops, JDP found the song he was looking for: "Where the Sidewalk Ends."

JDP initially released "Where the Sidewalk Ends" on his 2011 EP, *Purple*, and re-released it in his 2014 album, *In Pursuit: Side A*. The track is an introspective blend of dramatic instrumentals and modern rap, and is one of several songs available to discover on *Watch Dogs* through "Song Sneak." After finding it in the game, JDP streamed the song through his character's phone, hearing his own voice and music fill the gamespace of *Watch Dogs*' Chicago.

"That in itself was super surreal, it was awesome," said JDP. "Because it reminded me of when I was coming up and I played *Grand Theft Auto III* for the first time and was flipping through the radio stations. I was like, 'Man, what if I could get one of my songs in a game.' So it definitely was a great experience" (Pratt, 2015).

The come-up of Johnathan "JDP" Pratt began in Chicago's South Side. According to the artist, he grew up listening to a wide variety of music, blending influences from Frank Sinatra, Bob Dylan, LL Cool J, and Jay-Z into his own style. Perhaps most impressive of his journey

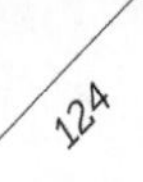

has been his autonomy as an artist. Everything JDP has accomplished has been done independently: working with an independent team, booking shows by himself, even rapping over original beats produced in-house. This DIY spirit was a great contributor to his success, as well as his ability to think outside the traditional artist path.

"When I started, I went to Columbia College," JDP said. "Before that, I was really just looking at it like I was going to make this music, put out this mix tape, and we're just going to pop just like that."

"I didn't really see a lot of other revenue streams, I didn't even know really there were that many revenue streams out there, or I didn't really look at those as something that's included in the mix of being an artist and a way for artists to generate income until I went to Columbia and took some licensing classes, some business classes, some entertainment law classes and things like that. That entire experience really opened my eyes, in terms of not only what the future of the music industry was looking like, but what possible avenues I could go down to ensure that I had a future [in] making music."

In 2009, JDP released the mixtape *Air Raid*, which secured the emerging artist a spot in *URB Magazine*'s 15th annual "Next 100" issue alongside Drake, Asher Roth, Theophilus London, and more (URB Magazine, 2009). Following *Air Raid*, JDP released *High Times* in 2010 and *Where Anything Goes Vol. 2* in 2011. Then, in fall 2011, JDP was featured in Coke Zero's "Make It Possible" campaign through Music Dealers, in which audiences across the globe videotaped themselves dancing to one of Coke's pre-selected songs. In this playlist, JDP was featured three times, including his song "Circa '87 feat. Adam Tensta," which was the most popular song for participants to sync to their user-generated videos. After the campaign's viral success, JDP performed at Music Dealers' CMJ Showcase in New York City's Thompson Hotel.

"Since then, I've been really working on the licensing side of things, focusing on the newer projects that I have coming up and working with other artists and producers," said JDP, whose next major placement came in spring 2012 when his song, "Beware The Wild Things" was featured on *Jersey Shore*. *The Real World* and *Keeping Up with the Kardashians* also licensed his music, encouraging the Windy City native to relocate to Los Angeles in 2012.

"Seeing the traction that [the Coke placement] had, seeing one of my songs played all over the world, and people interacting with the record, in a way that they wouldn't have if you just put it out before like another song," said JDP. "That definitely opened my eyes."

According to JDP, his songwriting process hasn't changed much despite his success in music licensing. He frequently described his process as "organic," and that he approaches songs as part of a larger story that he's trying to tell, in which every song is another chapter of that story. While JDP says he doesn't write music so that he can be licensed, it is one avenue of exposure and revenue that he frequently considers after the creative process concludes.

"Most importantly is how a record makes you feel, and I feel focusing on the emotion of the song also makes it easier for that song to be licensed," said JDP. "Because music supervisors go off of feelings as well, so I feel like it's easier if they're looking for a song that feels like 'this.' I can say, 'yeah, I have something that fits.' It's easier for me to send somebody a record like that, just based off of a feeling."

"Licensing isn't a driving force, like 'I have to make music so that it can be licensed.' No, but it definitely is something that goes into consideration in making a song when we finish it," said JDP, though he also said that these experiences have affected his process in a few ways.

"It's definitely changed in terms of the beats that I select. I don't like using samples as much. I really want to make my music as original as possible, and I do think about that for that aspect of it, because if my song is able to be licensed somewhere then I don't want them to have to worry about clearing the samples," said JDP. "And I do keep in mind the taste of the times when I'm creating also. It's not like first and forefront a driving force in my music. But as a modern artist, you do have to keep in touch with the modern day when you're working."

JDP wrote the song "Where The Sidewalk Ends" while living in Chicago's Pilsen neighborhood, just before his relocation to the West Coast. According to JDP, it was the first song written for the album *In Pursuit: Side A*, which was released in 2014 and produced by Swim Team Music. Before the album's official release, however, JDP was contacted by Music Dealers with a vague request to send "Where the Sidewalk Ends" to somebody for a video game that was based in Chicago.

"Maybe a week or two before the game came out, I figured out what exactly the song was for and what the opportunity was," said JDP, "[but] I didn't really know how big a deal it was until Traxxion from The Swim Team called me when I posted it on Instagram. He was like, 'Yo man, that's gonna be one of the biggest games of the year. I've been waiting for that game for like three years.'"

"So from there, we definitely made sure we did as many things as possible. We definitely went hard on social media, trying to let people know about when the game was going to come out. We went back in and updated websites, starting blasting it to anybody we knew to make sure they look out for it."

Ubisoft's *Watch Dogs* follows the storyline of a hacker hell-bent on revenge through a fictional Chicago in this pulse-pounding techno thriller. Like many modern video games, *Watch Dogs* includes spinoff content in the gameplay, such as its in-game music discovery app called "Song Sneak." Players use their character's mobile device to "steal" music from a passerby, and the more songs one takes, the more music one can listen to while playing.

Music discovery is a powerful passion point for many Chicagoans, and the abundance of fresh, independent music is one of the city's great cultural assets. An app like "Song Sneak" was an innovative way to truly engage players with *Watch Dogs'* immersive, Chicago-based setting. However, if players were to enjoy this app as fully as Ubisoft anticipated, the songs would have to be worth sneaking. Neither stock tracks, famous music, nor rehashed songs would do.

Based on the real-life app Shazam, "Song Sneak" included over 50 songs that players could steal and afterwards stream during the gameplay. To flavor that list with authentic up-and-coming music, Ubisoft contracted my company Music Dealers to provide a curated list of songs from its artist community. Music Dealers Creative Director Tim Lincoln reviewed the brief and provided a playlist of diverse songs that fit the sonic identity of the game and embodied the indie sound of Chicago's soundscape.

We licensed twelve songs from eleven independent artists for *Watch Dogs*, heightening the music discovery component of the game with real music from genuine emerging artists. Players went from searching for these songs in the game to doing so in real life, downloading and purchasing tracks that *Watch Dogs* originally introduced them to.

"I feel like they were going for authenticity when they were choosing songs," said JDP. "They were choosing songs that really conveyed what the game was about, what the feel was they were trying to go for, and they wanted to capture the essence of, if you were in Chicago what were you probably listening to? If you were listening to these artists, what was your favorite song? I definitely dug that."

"I was really happy that Tim went with 'Where the Sidewalk Ends,' because that was a very specific song that came from a really authentic place. It had a real story that I put in that record."

It would seem that fans of *Watch Dogs* felt the same way. Shortly after the game's release, players discovered the song on YouTube, where it was viewed several hundred times a day throughout the first months following the game's release with no prior promotion. From the success of the placement, JDP said he was able to repost the project back on iTunes, whereas before it was available solely as a free download. Tracking the downloads, subscriptions, and views revealed that his fanbase had grown far beyond his native Chicagoland, spanning all of the U.S. and stretching to global ears as distant as the Philippines.

"Having that song on *Watch Dogs* really generated a lot of buzz from people who were already fans of my music to brand-new people who had never heard of me who were from all over the world," said JDP. "You just see the impact of how much music can translate. Maybe people didn't understand what I was saying in the song, but they understand how it felt in that moment."

"It's definitely one of my favorite placements, and I'm also really happy that they picked that song, because that song is one of my purest. I'm not trying to make a pop song or a dance song here, I just wanted to express myself, what I was going through in that moment. So for the fact for the people at Ubisoft to get that, and the people that play *Watch Dogs* to get that, was super dope to me."

The two purest revenue streams that independent artists can have, JDP said, are licensing and touring. Due to the nature of music licensing, in which one placement might be experienced by millions of eager ears, the potential for exposure makes licensing "one of the best things you can focus on as part of your plan," said JDP.

"Artists aren't the only ones with fans," he continued. "Coke has fans. Brands have their own set of fans, and having your music side-by-side with that helps you attract those fans, because they're like, 'Oh man, these guys like this kind of music. This music conveys what this brand is about and now that I'm a fan of this brand, let me check out this artist and see what else he has.'"

"One of the things that I love about being an artist in this day and age is that we have so many options in terms of where we want to send our music, what we want to do with our music, how you can get your music heard. There are so many options for it. But one of the best ones, in my opinion, is licensing."

Jason Michael Paul Productions, Inc., Company Spotlight

Through the fifty-year-old evolution from 8-bit blips to the platinum-selling soundtracks of today's games, music in video games has become a creative mammoth of an industry that has changed the way consumers experience video games. Perhaps most importantly, video game music is no longer confined to the console and is extending the conversation with gamers from inside their homes into concert venues worldwide. Tracking their efforts of using and creating music, it has become clear to video game brands that a focus on music immersion is bringing tangible business results.

A focus on music immersion is bringing tangible business results

Gamers want more than just to game. They want a multi-channeled experience from the brands whose games they play. Music has become one of the pivotal ways for a video game brand to provide its audiences with that additional medium of engagement. Live activations, concerts, and tours have sprouted as a means of extending the engagement cycle beyond the end credits and into real life.

There are several concert producers of video game orchestras who craft live interpretations of video game music. This niche has grown into a prominent component of the video game music experience, drawing crowds like few traditional operatic performances do anymore.

Jason Michael Paul is among those trailblazers who has helped pave the path into the Wild West of music in games. Concert producer and founder of Jason Michael Paul Productions, Jason has helped changed the way gamers experience music beyond the console, delivering music both iconic and emotive into the real, physical world for all to experience hands-on. Most famously, Jason has produced "Dear Friends: Music from Final Fantasy," "Play! A Video Game Music Concert," and "Legend of Zelda: Symphony of the Goddesses," among others.

"I started getting into production [in my sophomore year in college], and never really looked back," said Jason. "When I finished college, I already had a job secured in production, working with clients such as Sony PlayStation and Sun Microsystems and other various Fortune 500 clients, but the biggest client was Sony PlayStation" (Paul, 2015).

According to Jason, PlayStation led him to aspirations as a video game producer, handling a lot of the corporate entertainment for PlayStation, including the company's E3 trade show booth to their sales meetings, among others. One of Jason's earliest milestones in bringing the gaming experience from the URL to the RL was when he was tasked to create from scratch the first totally interactive PlayStation store at the Metreon.

"Basically I was the project manager on that project, so I was in charge of everything that went into that store, from actually building it off-site in a warehouse, deconstructing it, and then installing it into the store," said Jason. "So as you can imagine there were a lot of firsts. We were the first ever to implement a software bar, which enabled customers to basically play the game before they purchased it, and that was something that we conceptualized and came up with."

At 25-years-old, Jason left for Los Angeles where he founded Jason Michael Paul Productions, and his first client was Square Enix, the makers of *Final Fantasy*. The production company handled most of their events, including the *Kingdom Hearts* launch and *Final Fantasy* events, working with renowned game execs Tetsuya Nomura and Shinji Hashimoto. All the while, Jason further established his relationship with the then-president of the U.S. operation, Jun Iwasaki.

"[Iwasaki] was very instrumental in helping me along my way and pretty much paved the way for the first-ever stateside 'Dear Friends: Music from Final Fantasy' video game music concert," said Jason. "Without him and Kyoko Yamashita, these projects would have never existed or happened. So really, those two were the ones who really were the visionaries who helped me bring video game music to the masses. They were the ones responsible for taking it out of just Japan and allowing me to bring video game music to the States. And that was where it really all started."

"I had an epiphany when I was dreaming up the idea of taking video game music and performing it live. I was in Costa Rica and I had a CD from *Final Fantasy*, put it into this massive sound system that we had set up for a stadium show that I was doing the sound for in Costa Rica, and we played that music through the PA and a lightbulb went off in head. I was like, 'I want to do this exact same thing, except the artist is going to be the video game. And I'm going to use the visual accompaniment, along with the music, to really tell the story."

According to Jason, these concerts yielded overwhelming success for the brand, including breaking news for being the first-ever video game music concert with visual accompaniment. The group performed with the Los Angeles Philharmonic and the LA Master Chorale, further pushing the envelope of how live video music game can be experienced.

"What was once thought of as muzak is now thought of as contemporary music that should be regarded as such, as phenomenal, and now see how it works," said Jason. "It definitely was an experience that put video game music on the map. [...] That was over ten years ago, so we've come quite a long way since then to where we are now."

Following the "Dear Friends: Music from Final Fantasy" success, Jason also produced "More Friends: Music from Final Fantasy," corresponded with the one-year anniversary of the first "Dear Friends" concert. According to a concert synopsis on the Square Enix page from composer Nobuo Uematsu, "Dear Friends" was originally conceived as a one-time event in Los Angeles. The concert reportedly sold out in three days and received a highly positive reception, which encouraged the brand to start a national tour featuring the music.

After the "Dear Friends" tour ended, Jason stopped working with the franchise and decided to "let Final Fantasy assume its own course." Square Enix continued its concert series, including "Distant Worlds: Music from Final Fantasy" (2007), "Distant Worlds II: More Music from Final Fantasy" (2010), and others. Jason, meanwhile, teamed with Thomas Böcker, a renowned and award-winning German producer more notable for his work on Symphonic Game Music Concerts, which is lauded for being the longest-running and the first of their kind outside of Japan. Böcker and Jason worked together for "Play! A Video Game Symphony," a concert series that featured music from video games that range from *Silent Hill* (1999) to *World of Warcraft* (2004). According to a JMP Productions 2009 press release, a live album CD and DVD was released as well.

"'Play! A Video Game Symphony' [...] was kind of a who's-who of video game composers," said Jason. "I think I had everyone there, from Mitsuda-san to Uematsu-san to Kondo-san, Jason Hayes, Jeremy Soule, Martin O'Donnell, Michael Salvatori. That was a very phenomenal experience that kind of spoke volumes on where video game music is going and where we're headed."

After "Play!," Jason pursued still more orchestral performances, including its sequel, "replay! Symphony of Heroes" and a series based on the popular Nintendo franchise, *The Legend of Zelda*. "Play!" featured music from several Nintendo games, including *Legend of Zelda*, *Super Mario*, and *Metroid*, spurring relations with the multinational consumer electronics company. Additionally, Nintendo composer Koji Kondo performed during a portion of the "Play!" 2006 premiere in Chicago, after which Nintendo and Jason maintained strong relations, he said.

In 2011, Nintendo celebrated the 25th anniversary of *The Legend of Zelda* franchise with a sonic boom. At its E3 press conference at the Nokia Theatre, the company unveiled *The Legend of Zelda: Skyward Sword* (2011) for the Wii, the release of which was underscored by a live performance by the Orchestra Nova San Diego as The Legend of Zelda 25th Anniversary Symphony. Jason Michael Paul Productions produced the E3 press event for Nintendo, at which point it was announced the company would produce three more anniversary concerts in London, LA, and Tokyo.

It was clear by now that the brand Nintendo was starting to see tangible results coming from not just investing in the immersive experience of quality music during gameplay, but they were extending the conversation and promotion of the brand by releasing the songs to take on a life of their own. Nintendo published *The Legend of Zelda 25th Anniversary Special Orchestra CD*, a collection of live performances of The Legend of Zelda 25th Anniversary Symphony. According to Nintendo, every copy in the initial production of Skyward Sword came packed with a copy of the CD, a clear indication they were seeing the impact of music on the business results (Nintendo, n.d.).

According to Jason, the response from the concerts was overwhelming. Every concert of the Anniversary Symphony was completely sold out and the shows were highly praised by reviewers. So positive were the effects, Nintendo and Jason Michael Paul Productions teamed up for a world tour of full-movement orchestral concerts that followed The Legend of Zelda 25th Anniversary Symphony. The series included three seasons, "The Legend of Zelda: Symphony of the Goddesses," "Second Quest," and "Master Quest," all of which feature music and video footage from the now 30-year-old franchise.

Why would Nintendo go through such great efforts to produce concerts around the world? They felt the results.

"If you're familiar with *The Legend of Zelda*, you know the music has always been an integral part of the game itself," said Jason. "Everything from some of the more iconic imagery, such as the harp [and] the ocarina, which are all key and very symbolic elements of the *Zelda* games. So I think the music and the game go hand-in-hand."

"Mr. Kondo's music has always been very deserving of symphonic treatment and it was way past due. Not only did we give it the symphonic treatment, but we also gave it a full-movement symphony. So for the first time ever in video game music history, we actually created a full-movement symphony devoted to *The Legend of Zelda*. So that is something I'm very proud of. The voice of *The Legend of Zelda* has always been the music."

The voice of The Legend of Zelda has always been the music

For a franchise that is nearly as old as the modern video game industry, *Zelda* has experienced almost every evolution of music in games. From its NES to its newest releases, music has always played a pivotal role in both gameplay and marketing. *Ocarina of Time* is a landmark in the application of diegetic music and in-game music interaction, in which players actually performed music in order to understand and control the gamespace, yielding an incredibly immersive experience. Because of the close relationship between game and music, as Jason explained, music has become an essential factor in the franchise's legacy. Its soundtracks are as iconic as the plot itself, and its themes are often cited as the most recognizable songs of all video game music.

Accordingly, it makes sense for Nintendo to leverage music beyond the console to extend its relationship with consumers after the end credits and in between game releases. Nintendo and Jason Michael Paul Productions bridged the gap between *Zelda's* fictional Hyrule and the real world. By continuing the gamer experience beyond the first screen, Nintendo accelerated its audience of already devoted customers along the consumer journey to becoming loyal brand advocates. So loyal, in fact, they appear in complete regalia of green tunics and Master Swords to Jason's "Symphony" shows, humming their favorite songs from the franchise that they've memorized for years.

"When you're making these branded experiences and these environments, the music is really important," said Jason. "When you walk into that room, you can immediately recognize some of those orchestral arrangements that we have as part of the walk-in. When you hear the drop of, for example in *Majora's Mask*, 'The Song of Time,' if you hear just the first couple notes, you're immediately transported back to the game."

Branded experiences like The Legend of Zelda orchestra concert series make fantasies like Hyrule a reality for their fans, evolve simple button-mashing into a multi-faceted experience, and cement video game titles like *Zelda* into immortal legacies.

chapter 5 Television

This might be a familiar scene for you …

Three Millennials sit in a bedroom watching TV.

The oldest, a 22-year-old college student visiting her family for a long weekend, leans against the wall atop her 16-year-old sister's floral-patterned bed. The sister sits beside her, cross-legged, while their 13-year-old brother is sprawled on the floor before them as they watch their favorite show, which just so happens to be an AMC original.

Their mother passes by the open bedroom door, admiring this rare scene of all three of her children enjoying some good old-fashioned TV time together, like the good old days.

Hardly.

The kids' noses are pressed against their laptops, phones, tablets, watches, and seemingly every other gadget imaginable, as they "watch" intently.

The reality is, there's a lot more that goes into watching TV these days.

The 13-year-old brother swipes the screen of his tablet, returning to the fanfiction forum for the fictitious band on the show. The thumb of the 16-year-old sister taps a blue circle on her cell phone sporadically, Shazamming every song. Each captured track is immediately added to one of six Spotify playlists she manages, each of which represents the music tastes of a different character on the show. The oldest daughter frantically taps away at her phone, tweeting at the show's music supervisor, with other fans, and the bands whose music was featured in that episode.

The twittersphere is abuzz. Live tweets paired with lyrics from the song being played on screen. Free downloads. Hashtag show. Hashtag band. Hashtag network.

As the closing scene fades and the credits roll, the jaws and electronics of all three siblings drop, desperately trying to Shazam the song that plays in the background during the heart-thumping, climactic season finale – a remastered cover of an '80s classic by a modern blues-folk band.

"That was it? That was the end?" the youngest asked in a meek voice once the television faded to black silence. He returned to his sister's tablet, enormous doubt weighing visibly on his young shoulders, as the 22-year-old looked at the dark screen of her phone, afraid to swipe it to life. The middle sister unplugged her earbuds from the phone's audio jack, increased the volume to its highest decibel, and streamed that final song through one of the show's curated Spotify playlists.

When the mother next walked past the bedroom, she peered incredulously through the door. The oldest daughter sat on the bed cradling her younger siblings, who have fought like animals since the former departed for college. Of course, they are capturing the moment via Shapchat with the song's melody blasting in the background.

This is the powerful new face of music and television, one which is becoming increasingly familiar with each new show. Despite its innovative façade, the state of music in television still bears resemblance to its early predecessors. In fact, the music of today's television industry continues to serve similar to the some of the foremost roles of music for radio programs – one of television's earliest precursors.

Just as in the case of this fictional group of siblings, families would gather around the radio set upon hearing the music cues of their favorite programs, one of the most prominent and foundational examples of sonic identity. This old concept has since developed into the theme song for shows – attracting ears to the show and immersing viewers into the sonic identity, and therefore the branded experience, of the program. As radio transitioned into television, and for a long time thereafter, U.S. consumers were limited to three providers of content: CBS, NBC, and ABC. This exclusivity was obviously great for both the networks and the shows, as its viewers were entirely captivated/trapped by any experience; however, for the consumer who values choice (as is the case with virtually every modern consumer), this system was far from ideal.

Today, there are endless networks, innumerable channels, thousands of shows, and even video-streaming platforms that create their own original content, thus shattering the gatekeepers of old and going head-to-head against traditional networks to fight for viewers. The division of power has shifted in favor of the consumer, once again further justification of the Social Empowerment theory as consumer expectations have stabilized at high level of demands that only the most creative and innovative content creators can provide. Now great for the modern consumer who wants choice, those trying to market a specific show on a specific network at a specific time must develop creative means of attraction to hook those ever-choosy viewers. Granted, with services like DVR and on-demand viewing, time of air is less important than it once was; however, networks still require live viewers in order to sell ad space, make money, and stay in business.

With all this clutter and endless content, the music supervisor has come to play a dominant role in attracting and sustaining the attention of viewers who might otherwise turn the channel or revert to another screen completely. Music executive Russell Ziecker has cracked the code on using the marketing power of music to increase live viewership by, in at least one scenario, 9%, as well as create massive immersion into shows like *Nashville* by integrating authentic music experiences into the stories to satisfy two pivotal passion points for viewers and extend the relationship between viewer and show long after the season by selling songs from the show. After achieving enough single sales to accumulate platinum status, supervisors have created an entirely new revenue stream for the network, ABC.

This is the future role of the music supervisor – one who is involved at every stage of the music process of a single story, whether its experience is in a television commercial, an on-screen performance, or ancillary touchpoints like singles or downloads. Russell and the *Nashville* team have raised the bar for the use of music in television, and they're only going to have to hustle harder if they want to keep young viewers engaged.

Regardless of the endless choices for content we now have, historically, and still contemporarily, music in television is preeminently meant to support the story on-screen. The music must speak to the viewer on an emotional level, immerse them into the character experience on-screen, and find the perfect song for the scene. Nowadays, however, many television music supervision experts also look to ways to attract more live viewers to the show by maximizing the marketing power of music and selecting music that not only supports the story, but also satisfies consumer passions and delivers an entire music experience separate to the show itself.

The role of the TV music supervisor has much more at stake than simply picking the right song. Today, the music is considered a character of the show, and music is starting to formalize as a clear marketing tool. Attracting consumers to view the show live, enhancing the experience of viewing through crafting an immersive experience, and extending the relationship and conversations between viewers after the show airs, music is being called upon to play an increasingly more valuable role – and the top supervisors are rising to the challenge.

Music strategy – using music to attract, immerse, and extend – is applied most clearly in the television industry. Music is used to attract consumers by crafting the perfect sonic identity and creating consistency for the promos that advertise the show. Music is used to immerse by perfecting the songs that play during the show, integrating music cues or themes into the script for the characters on screen to interact with. Music is used to extend the relationship between viewers and the show by using social media, web pages and more to continue the dialogue long after the credits roll.

Today, a music supervisor's job isn't just finding the right song. The same expectations that any marketing department are held accountable for, the modern music supervisor must also consider. How can they increase live viewership? How can they increase viewer experience? How can they increase social engagement with the show online? How can they find ways to make money off of the music they already own?

A consistent and deplorable situation has followed, however. Music supervisors are held to these standards, yet are too often called in at the eleventh hour to solve problems that would have otherwise never arisen had they been brought on during early development. My hope is that, through hearing the successes of several notable TV music supervisors, content creators will learn to invest in music supervision as early as script development in order to layer in music strategy at the onset. It will not only help the music industry, but it will make the world of entertainment even better for the consumer.

Supervisors today need to be thinking about a hundred different things at once. Whether they know it or not, there are many other departments that rely on the music supervisors to do a killer job. From the promo department to the producers and directors, from actors to legal and finance teams, and ultimately the consumer as well, the better the supervisor is at thinking ahead, the better everyone's experience becomes, and the easier it is for them all to do their jobs.

For instance, consider the promo departments. If they don't have a clear sense of the sonic identity of the show, it's harder for them to pick a song to use in the advertising of that show. If they're not picking a song with consistency that complements the show itself, they are not leveraging the full marketing power of music. That is what we sometimes refer to as divergent audio touchpoints: when two audio touchpoints, such as the promo commercial and the show itself, apply music strategy inconsistent to each other and thus weaken the overall sonic brand of the show. Conversely, when different audio touchpoints apply music strategy in parallel to each other, we call those convergent audio touchpoints, because two different audiovisual experiences are converging through music and sound. This strengthens the sonic identity of the show, which thus increases the show's overall brand, ultimately leading to a more immersive experience for the consumer.

The cleverest of supervisors will use this promo time to call out the music activity that will be taking place live during the show's air time. Russell Ziecker is leading the industry in this specialty.

Rather than use the promo time to do no more than say, more or less, "Be sure to watch this week's episode of *Nashville*, it's going to be awesome," his promos follow a different marketing strategy.

"Be sure to watch this week's episode of *Nashville*, we'll be releasing a brand new, never-before-heard single from such-and-such artist," the promos announce, though obviously in different words. While this difference may seem minimal, that focus on music resulted in a 9% increase in live viewership. On top of that, the song hits all aspects of music strategy: attraction, immersion, and extension.

The song hits all aspects of music strategy: attraction, immersion, and extension

Russell's music strategy attracted 9% more viewers to watch the show live. It immersed them into the experience as the music was authentic to and integrated throughout the plot of the show. It extended the relationship with the viewers as fans tweeted and shared the song on social media in the days following the airing, and through Shazam they were able to receive a free download of the song that they could listen to and harken back to *Nashville* long after the season ended. Furthermore, the sonic identity of *Nashville* that Russell's team had expertly cultivated throughout the season resulted in a new revenue stream for ABC in the form of monetizable music, the aggregate sales of which met Platinum record standards.

Russell has cracked the code of music supervision and done the impossible – proved a return on investment for music used in television. Let's break down the details of how this all works. While music supervision is not a color-by-number formula – in fact, it is an art and a craft, the execution of which can never be strictly duplicated from one project to another – there are nonetheless core functions that music strategy should always aim to execute, and ten key audio touchpoints by which a music supervisor can apply that strategy. This is the closest we can come to formulizing an artistic process, which is important in order to link results between music and sales for networks to invest more money into music departments, music supervisors, and into the music industry.

Here are the ten audio touchpoints of the television industry, all of which Russell and his team for *Nashville* maximized in order to deliver the most engaging experience to viewers.

1. Sonic Identity: The consistent sonic identity of *Nashville* provided viewers with a sense of trust in the curatorial prowess of the show, meaning they could watch it live each week and leave with a new song or artist who they otherwise would not have discovered on their own.
2. Promo Commercials: By promoting both the show and the music of the show in its promos, *Nashville* appealed to both consumer passion points – story and music – in order to attract viewers to watch the next episode.
3. Title Sequence: The opening credits for the show echo the sonic identity of *Nashville*'s setting.
4. Non-Diegetic Syncs: The background music of the show immersed viewers into the show and provided Russell and the music supervisor for the show with unique opportunities to connect new artists.
5. Diegetic Syncs: Few shows execute diegetic music like *Nashville* did, as the show integrated music into its story and provided viewers with live performances by the cast each episode.
6. Social Media: The social media profiles of the show amplified the music story of the show to extend the experience beyond the first screen.
7. Web Page: ABC Family has a music page, ABC Music Lounge, where its music is housed, including artist interviews and exclusive content.
8. Artist Relationships: By working with artists, *Nashville* coordinated timed releases and cross-promotional opportunities.
9. Monetizable Assets: The music of *Nashville* was available for purchasable download, the sum of which was thus used to contribute to the overall value of music strategy.
10. Live Activation: A live tour even followed the show's airing, which was televised as well as corollary content.

Russell Ziecker is one of several music supervisors who maximized the marketing power of music to create the most engaging experiences for viewers. Here following are the case studies of Russell and others who are revolutionizing music supervision in television, teasers of which have been published in my eBook, *The Marketing Power of Music: Music + Television*.

Music Supervision Today

(*with John Houlihan and Jonathan McHugh, President and Secretary, Guild of Music Supervisors*)

"A qualified professional who oversees all music related aspects of film, television, advertising, video games, and any other existing or emerging visual media platforms as required."

This is a partial definition of the music supervisor according to the website of the Guild of Music Supervisors, which was founded in 2008 by some of the industry's top music supervisors. Among the group's goals, according to the site, is to "take a leadership position with one galvanized voice in the entertainment industry" – an ambition that it will continue to fulfill as the role of music in media evolves (Guild of Music Supervisors, n.d.).

"The Guild was formed because the modern version of music supervision has really only been around since the late-80s, which is when the need for music supervisors kind of exploded," said John Houlihan, President of the Guild and veteran music supervisor. "But it's been kind of a Wild West, and there wasn't much infrastructure or support for supervisors, or any clarity in the industry" (Houlihan, 2015).

According to Houlihan, a prospective guild member must meet a certain amount of music supervisor credits on commercially released content in order to join. In each division of music supervision – including television, film, games, and more – different criteria determine the number of necessary credits a supervisor must hold to ensure he or she is adequately experienced in the trade. The Guild also offers several events each year so members may network, interact, share experience, and help solve problems.

Despite the reality of being competitors in an already competitive industry, music supervisors have assembled through the Guild both to help each other and to advance their shared craft.

"The purpose of the Guild is to uplift and uphold the quality of the craft, and we just need to make sure that all of our members are experienced and ethical, and would be members that will help us all form an experienced collective to help uplift the true craft of music supervision," said Houlihan.

A profession with roots dating back to the days when theaters provided live music to accompany silent films, the role and responsibilities of music supervision have undergone tremendous change in the past few decades. Technology, an expansion of audio touchpoints, a global upsurge in music appreciation and consumption, the content-driven landscape of modern consumerism – all of the topics explored in this book, and more, have contributed to this revolutionized form of music supervision.

However, not everyone understands the evolution of the craft, leaving it up to others to inform them of this important transition.

"I organized a panel for the Producers Guild during their annual conference where we brought out the producers and music supervisors of big films and TV shows like *The Descendants* and *Parenthood*," said Guild Secretary and seasoned supervisor, Jonathan McHugh. "We talked about how music influenced the story. Producers and directors are the ones who hire us; without them, we don't work. So we must educate them to what we do and how important our craft is and why they should hire quality, bonafide music supervisors" (McHugh, 2015).

According to McHugh, music and music supervisors are frequently the lowest parts of a production's budget. So, when a film or a TV show shoots, the other departments will often look to cutting music as a way to save money. For some smaller productions, it's even the music supervisor who will get cut.

"Our craft is in danger, and we need to support it," said McHugh, who explained that reconnecting with publishers, music libraries, record labels, and artists after a placement helps all parties maintain a strong presence in the realm of music supervision.

Ingrid Michaelson, for example, has had her songs successfully synced by numerous music supervisors in a variety of placements. She performed at a Guild fundraiser in November 2014 (ASCAP, n.d.).

Michaelson, an indie-folk/pop singer-songwriter with six albums, began her music career by streaming her music via Myspace. It wasn't until a music producer from ABC's *Grey's Anatomy* reached out to the artist that Michaelson's audience expanded to millions. "Breakable," from her second album, *Girls and Boys*, was featured on episode 3:08 of *Grey*'s in 2006. Shortly after, the artist re-released the album with the marketing and distribution support of Original Signal Recordings. It peaked at #63 on Billboard 200 and sold nearly 300,000 copies. Since then, Michaelson has had credits on 28 different television shows, and her music has appeared in 14 episodes of *Grey's Anatomy*. So influential to the show's music strategy, the sync of her song, "Into You," in the season premiere was voted "#1 Music Moment of Grey's Anatomy Season 9" (ABC, n.d.a.).

Despite the vast potential of music, TV shows, films, and audiovisual projects of all types sometimes don't hire a music supervisor until the end. According to Houlihan, supervisors will often get brought in at post-production, "and a lot of those jobs are cleaning up a mess and getting the project out of problems that they can't get themselves out of before they hired a music supervisor."

Most, if not all, music supervisors agree that a music supervisor's involvement should start in pre-production with the script. Because music may play a role in the storyline, the music supervisor helps coordinate music–plot integration into the script. On-camera music issues are handled during the shoot, and sync licensing extends all the way through the final mix of the production. And when music is leveraged in the marketing of the production, the music supervisor is likely to stick around even longer.

A music supervisor's involvement should start in pre-production with the script

"I'll sometimes also put the music together into a compilation and put it out, and so then I'm attached to it forever, in a way, because you're obviously trying to help the marketing of that movie all down the road," said McHugh, who's produced nearly fifty soundtracks for film and TV. "So you're always looking at it to find the best music, but also to find something that has trajectory. [...] You're looking to find that song that's going to be popular by the time that your movie comes out."

Such are the mental processes of music supervisors and music agencies. A placement is more than a scene that needs background sound. A song is more than its originally recorded version. And music strategy is more than syncing a song and calling it a day. Part of music strategy is determining how to best leverage music in and out of the production – even after it airs. In fact, it's often the music that can keep the conversation going and extend the viewer relationship with the show.

Licensing music with this creative foresight is evidence of the sophistication of the music supervisor's craft. As with any other profession, however, there are tools of the trade that must be readily available in order for a supervisor to best serve the music needs of the show.

"We need to network with licensing people, and people like yourselves [Music Dealers], because you guys could save our lives," said

McHugh. "[If] we need a piece of music, at the last minute on the stage and it has to get cleared, we need to have a relationship with you or the publisher or the record company and we can call at 8 pm on Friday night and go, 'Hey I need you to clear this song right now.' That is the currency for us."

Managing music expenses is another chief responsibility of the music supervisor, and one that is often mishandled when a production opts to not hire an expert supervisor. These decisions are often made when planning the budget for a film, during which an inexperienced film producer may look at the project's music budget, see a $75,000 fee for music supervisors, and think that the money would be better suited going towards licensing more songs. According to Houlihan, such choices are poor mistakes, because a good music supervisor will earn back their fee and more in savings.

"Our typical challenge is to deliver a million-and-a-half dollars' worth of market value music licenses to a film on a $500,000 music licensing budget. So how do we do that?" said Houlihan. "We do that with skilled negotiation, with using our powerful contacts, with creative solutions, and we use it with our experience of working with a set of filmmakers and the studio."

"An inexperienced producer might look at a music supervisor fee as an expense, but a seasoned, experienced film producer will look at that and recognize the value that the music supervisor is going to add and the savings that they're going to get overall in the process. It's a very good, strategic spend of your money to bring in someone experienced to keep you from hitting any icebergs," said Houlihan.

"Having someone on the team that can get to artists, find brand-new stuff that's going to blow up, and get the best possible prices on songs [...] is super important," agreed McHugh. "We deal with everybody, and our job is to know as many people as possible to help make the music in the [production] great."

Nashville's Other Music Star

(*with Russell Ziecker*)

As Executive Vice President of Television Music at Lionsgate, Russell Ziecker oversees Lionsgate's music department and its numerous facets, including licensing, staffing of individual shows, and all of the company's television productions. Ziecker has produced the music for over 400 commercials, has worked on nearly 600 singular episodes of television, and has credits on nearly 40 TV shows, including ABC's *Nashville*.

Based on fictional country music stars, *Nashville* naturally required expert music management in order to produce an authentic, engaging show. In February 2015, the show's premier music strategy earned its music supervisor, Frankie Pine, a win in the "Best Music Supervision – TV Comedy or Musical" category at the Guild of Music Supervisors Awards.

As head of television music, Ziecker works with numerous shows on varying levels of supervision for each, including crafting the sonic identity of shows before the pilot episode even airs. During many of these sonic deliberations, Ziecker is coming up with the right style of music for a scene by working only from the script. Ziecker and Lionsgate have frequently been tapped by networks during brand relaunches when the networks repositioned themselves as places for original content. Examples of this include his work on *Weeds* for Showtime, *Mad Men* for AMC, *Deadbeat* for Hulu, *The Royals* for E!, *Boss* for STARZ, and *Manhattan* for WGN.

"My responsibilities lie in the flavoring of the show, more than mnemonics," explained Ziecker. "We help brand the shows and find their initial voice before they go to air" (Ziecker, 2014).

Once that show does air, the sonic identity that was crafted before its launch must be maintained with a carefully supervised music strategy.

For *Nashville*, this includes choosing which songs to license for use in the show, which songs they want to create as originals, as well as deciding how to feature them.

Typically, music cues are non-diegetic: music synced as background sound or mood music to build the emotions of the scene. More often now in television, and especially in *Nashville*, the music is diegetic: music whose source is presented as part of the story space.

For a show like *Nashville*, the plot of which lives entirely in the music industry, its sonic identity and resulting music strategy are greatly defined by its diegetic syncs. The music that its characters perform, compose, and even enjoy listening to is a definitive part of the show. Therefore, each song must be selected with meticulous attention to a number of factors in order for it to be the right fit.

"[One example of this included] the two little girls on our show, Lennon and Maisy Stella, who play the daughters of Rayna Jaymes. In our storyline, we had Rayna Jaymes playing at an arena in New York, and she has the girls up on stage to do a soundcheck," Ziecker explained. "We needed the right [song] that the girls' mom, Rayna Jaymes the country star, would have known. We needed something that our audience demographic [...] would have known. So it sort of had to be something off the charts at the time, and something that the girls would have found cool and adapt it to their own style."

A huge part of *Nashville*'s intrigue is its unique use of diegetic music. Not only is the background music a powerful component of the show's character: the actors even perform in the show, sometimes creating new songs for the scene, and at other times covering well-known songs with a creative twist. In this episode, *Nashville* would employ the latter strategy and work with the Stella sisters to produce a unique version of a popular track.

This would be the girls' second on-screen performance in the series, the first being an acoustic cover of *Nashville*'s first radio single,

"Telescope" by Hayden Panettiere (Juliette Barnes on the show). Having won the attention of viewers with their first performance, as well as becoming YouTube sensations before being casted for the show, the Stella sisters were bound to captivate viewers again during their soundcheck scene – as long as the right song was selected.

"At first, we poked around and we played around with Mumford and Sons' 'I Will Wait,'" said Ziecker, but the song was reportedly not available to them at that time. "[The show] was filming the next day, [so] we needed a track right away. We had come up with The Lumineers' 'Ho Hey,' had the girls cut it that night with Buddy Miller [*Nashville*'s music producer], and we used it in the show the next day."

"It was perfect. It was our biggest downloaded song [and] reached 140,000 [downloads]. So, that was one [occurrence when the song] had to connect with story, had to be something current and new, and that everybody knew."

By covering The Lumineers' "Ho Hey," Nashville increased engagement with its audience by repurposing a song whose popularity had seemingly peaked, reviving it with a fresh adaptation to give the existing hit a second life lending a nice hand to the music industry.

Give the people what they want. It's an age-old paradigm, and something that every TV show strives to do with its content. But to give people something they can't get anywhere else – that's something else entirely. That's the art of marketing with music.

Nashville is renowned for lining its episodes with original music. Since that first radio single, "Telescope," which peaked at 33 on Billboard's Country Airplay chart, the show has consistently produced custom songs that look, sound, and feel as real as any other country hit. That authenticity isn't coincidental, nor is it always the case with original music.

The key to authenticity lies in the hands of the artist, as Ziecker and the music team on *Nashville* prove time and time again. Real artists who write real songs, with heart and artistic deliberation, are the only types of musicians who can accomplish this feat. Lucy Schwartz, for her work on *Nashville*, is living proof of this point.

An LA-based singer/songwriter, Schwartz has released three albums and two EPs on her own independent label, Fortunate Fools Records (Schwartz, n.d.). Several months after the release of her latest album, *Timekeeper*, Ziecker and Pine spoke with Schwartz about writing a song for *Nashville* and discussed the show's upcoming storyline and character trajectories.

"Lucy delivered three songs," Ziecker said. "She thought the first one was definitely the one to use: she had a character in mind. And same with the second one. For the third one, she said, 'You know, this reminded me of *Nashville*, and you can have it. But, if you don't use it, I'm just going to use it on my record.' And it was a song called 'Black Roses.'"

In the thirteenth episode of season two, *Nashville* character Scarlett O'Connor penned the poignant lyrics in her journal as a poem. Later in the episode, Scarlett's mother – the motivation behind the haunting lyricism – makes a dramatic appearance on the show. Portrayed by actress Clare Bowen, Scarlett then performs and records "Black Roses," *Nashville*'s featured song of that week.

"There was a lot of tension between the two characters, and this was the perfect song lyrically and just told that storyline better than anything else we'd found," said Ziecker. "The song and the way it was used in the episode really had an emotional impact on the viewers."

Ancillary touchpoints: music that extends

"These are songs that you've never heard before. They've never been released in any way," said Ziecker, speaking to *Nashville*'s soundtrack of original music. "We're pulling directly from the music community that we portray on television, and we're putting it in the hands of our cast, in the mouths of our cast, which results in having the singles available to download."

Downloadable singles are one of many ways to build consumer engagement and extension outside of a show's airtime. As mentioned before, viewers will only become supporters when they're given something worthwhile. Hearing high-quality, original music in an episode and being able to download it immediately afterwards does exactly that.

According to Ziecker, *Nashville* recently hit 4 million total downloads on its songs, all of which can be accessed through the network's music site, ABC Music Lounge. The site showcases everything about the music that's featured on ABC's shows, including music videos, performance footage, and exclusive interviews with the artists and music supervisors. ABC have realized the marketing power of music to immerse viewers and extend the relationship, turning a normal viewer into an advocate of their content and network.

When episode 2:13 aired, the network led a promotion on Music Lounge that allowed viewers to download "Black Roses" for free. The single was downloaded 80,000 times just that night and later reached No. 6 on the iTunes Country charts. Additionally, the song was featured on the album, *The Music of Nashville: Original Soundtrack Season 2, Volume 2*. (ABC, n.d.b.)

Perhaps most notable is the lifespan of "Black Roses." When ABC Music Lounge launched its documentary web series, "On the Record," which followed the life of *Nashville*'s original songs from inception to on-air premiere, Schwartz was interviewed with Pine and Bowen about "Black Roses." The web series led up to a televised concert at Nashville's famous Ryman Theatre, where *Nashville*'s cast performed original songs from the show to a live audience. Bowen performed "Black Roses," earning a standing ovation, and was later joined by Schwartz for an acoustic performance of the song.

Finally, ABC uploaded all of this content – downloads, exclusive videos, and interviews – to Music Lounge, along with a short biography on Schwartz and both the lyrics and piano tabs to "Black Roses" (ABC, n.d.b.).

"I think ABC does a good job [...] with Music Lounge by keeping music an integrated, but separate experience [for viewers]," said Ziecker. "Somewhat discouraging is knowing the power [some providers] have in this medium of digital platforms, but because their infrastructure has had to adapt so quickly and move so quickly, there's no music mechanism put in place yet, where they could either monetize the music or help promote the music that's [in their shows]."

Because of his tremendous experience in both the music and television industries, Russell Ziecker is able to look at his work from multiple angles: a macro and a micro viewpoint. On one hand, Russell focuses on how music can increase engagement in a television show, evidenced by how carefully he, Frankie Pine, and *Nashville*'s team select songs for use in the show. The right song choice, synced to the right scene, and performed in the right way – like The Lumineers' "Ho Hey" – can define a character for the remainder of the series.

This creates a bond with the viewer that extends far beyond how one traditionally regards a television show. It evolves into a deeper relationship, one in which the viewer trusts the program to consistently deliver high-quality, brand-new music. The more helpful a show can be in the process of music discovery, the more important it becomes to the viewer. Consumers, across all demographics and industries, seek to be trend-setters rather than followers; therefore, music discovery can be a very powerful tool in influencing the behaviors of a show's audience.

And on the other hand, Russell (and ABC through its Music Lounge site) pays attention to the needs and abilities of the artist community of the show. Lucy Schwartz is one stunning example of how strongly placements can influence an artist's music career. Lucy, and all of the other wonderful songwriters who contribute original songs for television, can then receive substantial revenue as writers, publishers, and/or performers of the music. The evolving way that TV shows like *Nashville* are using music in turn benefit the music industry by providing artists an additional revenue stream that fills the gaps left by streaming and sales.

Shameless Syncs for a Sonic Identity

(*with Ann Kline*)

After working as an attorney in the music department at William Morris Agency, Ann Kline has since garnered credits on 39 different projects and hundreds of TV episodes as music supervisor. These include over 150 episodes of *The West Wing* and over 130 episodes of *Third Watch* in the early 2000s.

Most notable, perhaps, is Kline's recent work on the Chicago-based comedy-drama, *Shameless*. In February, Kline earned a nomination at the Guild of Music Supervisors Awards in the "Best Music Supervision – Television Comedy Or Musical" category for her work on the show.

Frequently lauded for its soundtrack, which includes everything from Vegas-born surf-rock band Rusty Maples to LA-based indie-rock duo The Peach Kings, the Showtime original has a sonic identity that is heavily rooted in up-and-coming music. According to Kline, this decision was made early on and was based on the tone of *Shameless*' storyline.

"I spent a lot of time sitting with John Wells and Mark Mylod, the executive producers, trying all different things to figure out what kind of score we wanted," said Kline. "We were thinking that we would hire a rock band to score the show, because it's such a messy, kind of rebellious, young-feeling show" (Kline, 2014).

The main characters of *Shameless* – the Gallagher family – are mostly young adults and adolescents growing up in a neighborhood on

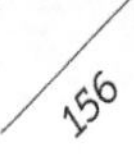

Chicago's South Side. Accordingly, the music had to reflect the real tastes of urban youth to create a real experience for viewers. Only authentic music could accomplish this.

"So we started playing around with scoring it with these independent rock bands' music, and it worked out so well that we ended up just licensing the music and [did] it episode to episode," continued Kline. "And still along the way we thought eventually we were going to hire a composer."

Shameless will occasionally license a track from a production music library; however, to truly benefit from the marketing power of music, the majority of the songs featured in each episode are from real, active artists. Authentic, indie music simply syncs better with the sonic identity of the show. The artists that decidedly remain independent and choose to not sign with a major label further enforces the identity of the characters and the show. This provides *Shameless* with the opportunity to market the music of the show, as it creates another layer in the communication with its audience. Accordingly, the consumer engagement potential of the show's marketing efforts skyrocket with new possibilities.

A strong example of how well real indie music can support a show is in the title sequence for *Shameless*. The show's theme song is "The Luck You Got" by The High Strung, a garage-rock/pop band from Detroit. First featured on the band's independently released album, *Moxie Bravo*, "The Luck You Got" showcases a strong indie vibe with punchy lyrics – an apt sync for *Shameless*.

"Themes for TV are really difficult to find because you're looking for something that people won't get sick of episode after episode and that really captures the vibe of the show," said Kline. "We went back and forth between some other songs and different versions of what the main title sequence was going to look like. Once we saw ['The Luck You Got'] with the picture, it was like, 'We're done, this is it.'"

The title sequence of *Shameless* depicts the Gallagher family bathroom, wherein a montage of scenes from the family's life plays. Drinking, smoking, and much, much more – all while "The Luck You Got" plays almost sarcastically in the background.

According to Kline, the song was initially deemed the best pick for the sync based on how well it fit with the sonic identity of the show. Its lyrics, instrumentals, and vocals all fit the grungy, ironic theme of *Shameless*. However, as an up-and-coming indie band, The High Strung was also an appropriate artist to license and work with for mutual benefit.

"I think the main title sequence is a good example of that," Kline said. "It airs every week and I think it's great for us and great for the band. This song is one that no one's ever heard before and it's a big main title sequence that shows don't really have anymore. So, it's great exposure for them and great exposure for us."

The licensing of an emerging band like The High Strung offers a show a lot of potential marketing leverage, because then that show also has access to the band's audience. Up-and-coming artists are much more likely to promote the fact that their song was licensed for a TV show than a major-label artist or even a production studio of in-house composers. Beyond the payment the bands receive for the license, major placements give indie artists the professional recognition that affirms their art and hard work. For up-and-comers, placements are career milestones, and they want to share that experience with the fans who helped secure their success by believing in them from the ground up.

For popular major artists, a placement might be just one of many checks, none of which would likely be promoted without being paid an even larger check. This is not the case with most indie artists, as they are relying more and more on syncs to go mainstream.

"We see the most of that on *Shameless* because the bands will contact us and say, 'Thank you so much, so many people told me that

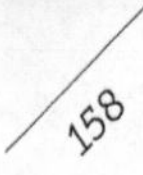

they heard my song on *Shameless*, and that's how they found the album,'" said Kline. "I think it feeds from the bands' websites and other social media outlets. They will say, 'This song was featured in *Shameless*,' and it will work the other way and we could get viewers from their fanbase."

There's no better highlight of the attraction power of music than people tuning into a show because of wanting to hear their favorite band on TV. It provides a certain level of cool for listeners to feel like they discovered a band, and now the rest of the world is catching on there's a 'stamp of approval' because they were placed in a show.

To that point, The High Strung features three *Shameless* plugs right at the front of their site: a blurb that boasts, "Our song 'The Luck You Got' is the theme song on the new Showtime series, *Shameless*"; the trailer for the show embedded from YouTube; and a free download for fans of "'The Luck You Got' from Showtime series *Shameless*" (The High Strung, n.d.).

Additionally, as a form of immersion and extension, Showtime lists all of the music featured on the show and links directly to the artist's site or iTunes page, according to Kline.

"When I first started, back in the '90s, there was not a lot of music in television at all," said Kline. "It wasn't like this platform for showcasing music, and I think over the years it's become such a synergistic relationship where the TV shows can help showcase the artists and the artists can help bring viewers to the TV show."

Concluding thought

Ann Kline's work on *Shameless* is a clear example of how real, authentic music is often the stronger alternative to licensing stock tracks from production libraries or even famous artists. As she explained, television can be a platform for music discovery, which is a very powerful statement to make. This means that two very different mediums – music and television – are coming together for the benefit of both industries. TV shows are helping artists, artists are helping TV shows, and consumers are benefitting by being able to count on these TV shows to deliver the newest, most cutting-edge music each week. Bands that viewers would never have discovered otherwise are introduced in tandem with the story's evolving plot, providing a bonus incentive which attracts viewers to tune in regularly.

Ann's tendency to work with indie artists for *Shameless* is an extension of this trend. In many cases, the more up-and-coming the artist is, then the more they'll want to cross-promote with the show. Other supervisors will experience the same effect when they put such careful thought into what type of music they choose to license.

Dark, Sexy, & Bloody: The Music of *True Blood*

(*with Gary Calamar*)

Honoree of "Music Supervisor of the Year (Television)" by the Guild of Music Supervisors in 2011, co-author of the 2010 book *Record Store Days*, five-time Grammy-nominated TV/film music supervisor, long-time DJ at KCRW, and one of the coolest people I know – Gary Calamar is a legendary name in music supervision.

President of music services company Go Music, Calamar has earned credits on over 45 different projects and has supervised the music on some of the most acclaimed shows on television, including *Six Feet Under*, *Entourage*, *Weeds*, and more. Gary was the first TV supervisor in LA to sit me down and teach me some of the tips of successful music supervision and where I learned a lot about the power of music in television. You'd be hard pressed to find such an accomplished but nice person, and I'm thrilled to be able to share some of his teaching with you.

Of the many shows Calamar has had the responsibility of shaping with sound, his work with HBO's famed vampire soap opera, *True Blood*, is among his most distinguished.

According to Calamar, one of his first duties for *True Blood* was to replace the theme song, which creator Alan Ball selected when he was writing the episodes for the pilot season. Calamar says Ball would frequently browse iTunes during writing spells, and at one point stumbled upon "Bad Things" by Jace Everett. Ball reportedly liked it, downloaded it, and started using it temporarily as the theme song for *True Blood*.

"And when [Ball] brought me in, that was the first mission of mine, to find the theme song of the show," said Calamar. "['Bad Things'] was the placeholder and it was nice, but maybe it was a little too humorous or something. We had some people write some things for us, and I tried a bunch of different things that seemed close, but as time went on we realized that 'Bad Things' was kind of perfect" (Calamar, 2014).

Everett's haunting baritone guides the country tune. The ominous lyrics, Everett's vocals, and the bayou-drenched, country-rock texture of "Bad Things" all reflect the gritty attitude of *True Blood*.

"I kind of used that as a template for the sound of the show; it had just the right mixture of danger and menace and humor and sexiness," said Calamar. "A couple of times I would bring in some fairly serious songs for Alan to try out, and he was like, 'this is a show about vampires, let's have some fun with this.'"

"That helped me develop the sound of the show. And certainly the region, the Louisiana sound, was certainly a big part of the sound of the show, and the darkness and the humor and the sexiness. To me, it all stemmed from 'Bad Things.'"

The music strategy of *True Blood* leans heavily on this first sync. Everett's distinct style would inform each music decision for the remainder of the series, encapsulating the sonic identity of the show with "Bad Things." And while the show owes much of its success to Everett's song, the artist can also attribute some of his success to *True Blood*.

Though "Bad Things" was released as a single in 2005, it wasn't until it aired as the theme song for *True Blood* that the song received international recognition. In 2009, it ranked second on Norway's VG-lista and appeared on Sweden's national record chart and UK Singles. Additionally, it won a BMI award in 2009 in the cable television category and was nominated for "Best Scream Song of the Year" in 2009 for Spike TV's Scream Awards, all showing the value that Calamar's supervision brought back to the music industry (Everett, n.d.).

Because of *True Blood*, millions of viewers were exposed to "Bad Things." When shows syndicate across networks or are licensed to media-streaming sites like Netflix or Hulu, that number multiplies immeasurably. Compared to record deals or radio plays, television placements can offer artists much greater reach and exposure, leading to the widely held belief that music licensing is now among the top ways for artists to break.

Everett's success highlights this trend and explains why music supervisors are often considered an artist's greatest ally in the industry.

Investing in long-term relationships with artists is a practice employed by skilled music supervisors. During *True Blood*, Calamar launched a partnership with Louisiana native C.C. Adcock, and brokered a relationship that would benefit both parties immensely over the following years.

According to Calamar, Adcock introduced himself once he learned that *True Blood* would be filmed in Louisiana. Adcock, acclaimed for his Cajun swamp-pop and blues-influenced style, shared his knowledge of the area's rich musical history with Calamar. Shortly thereafter, the first episode of *True Blood* was shot, and featured the song, "Y'all'd Think She'd Be Good 2 Me" from Adcock's 2004 album, *Lafayette Marquis*.

Adcock was a tremendous resource to the show, according to Calamar, and has also proven to be very influential to the music industry at large. An advocate for the preservation of swamp pop music, Adcock co-founded the south Louisiana supergroup Lil' Band of Gold, and co-produced the 2009 documentary, *Promised Land: A Swamp Pop Journey* which premiered at South by Southwest and was screened at the Cannes film festival (IMDB, n.d.). So entrenched in the music that would partially define *True Blood*, Adcock was frequently tapped by Calamar for sync licensing, as well as an on-screen performance.

"So when it came time, at the end of the first season we were going to have a live band playing in Merlotte's, [Adcock] was the first choice," said Calamar. "He's totally fit [the show] in all ways, so it was an easy decision to make."

C.C. Adcock & The Lafayette Marquis performed five songs in the show's tenth episode – "Maison Creole," "Bleed 2 Feed," "I'm Just A Fool To Care," "I'm Ready," and "Let's Talk It Over" – during the engagement party of characters Arlene and Rene.

"I think we always, on *True Blood*, have a good budget and a good feel for how the music should be," said Calamar. "And we want to have the real thing in there. But I work on other projects where we had actors pretending they were playing, and that could work as well, but we actually wanted to have the real thing in there [on *True Blood*]."

"So, we were able to find the budget to bring him and his band over," said Calamar. "It was a bit of an expense, and made it a bit more difficult, but we ended up having some live tracks that we had available online, and I think it just makes it more authentic to do it that way."

As a form of marketing extension and monetization, all four of the songs appear on the show's soundtrack album for its first season, though three are only available as bonus tracks on the deluxe edition. "Bad Things" joins as the album's opening track. Released on the same day as the DVD and Blu-ray releases of season one, *True Blood*'s original soundtrack received a 2010 Grammy nomination for best compilation soundtrack album, showing the extension power of music to continue the conversation of a show, after the credits roll (HBO, n.d.).

The difference between hiring actors that portray artists and licensing real, active artists can be huge. The former offers no additional benefits for the show, whereas working with authentic musicians can create completely new verticals through which the show can be promoted. In *True Blood*'s case, it brought on real artists for in-scene performances, which then provided the show with bonus tracks that led to a Grammy nod. That's the art of marketing with music.

True Blood has earned Grammy nominations on three of its four soundtracks, which feature music from six of the show's seven seasons. Much of the soundtracks' acclaim comes from the show's covers of famous songs, including "She's Not There" by The Zombies (HBO, n.d.).

Each episode of *True Blood* is named after a song, which immediately reveals how much the show values music. According to Calamar, these widely popular covers began first with the writer of each episode. Most often, the writers will reportedly have a particular song in mind as they develop the scene, and this song will reflect some part of that episode's storyline. For example, episode 4:10 closes with a crowd of vampires stalking towards their rivals' home with rocket launchers. For that episode, Calamar synced The Used's cover of "Burning Down the House" by Talking Heads.

"The first episode [of season six] was going to be, 'Don't Let Me Be Misunderstood,'" said Calamar of another example. "They wanted to put in The Animals' version of the song. I said, 'You know, we've got some time, maybe we can do a new version of that. The old version by The Animals is great, but it'd be nice to bring it up to date and freshen it up a little bit.'"

Calamar paired Eric Burdon, vocalist for The Animals, with singer-songwriter Jenny Lewis, the former vocalist for the indie-rock band Rilo Kiley, for the master refresh. Between the enduring roar in Burdon's voice and Jenny's sultry vocals, their cover of "Don't Let Me Be Misunderstood" echoes the dark, sexy themes that *True Blood* touts.

That episode, however, never aired, and the song never made it to screen. Nonetheless, HBO uploaded the cover to YouTube, where it's since earned over 100,000 views (Atorecords, n.d.). Additionally, it was one of the most popular songs on the show's soundtrack, *True Blood: Music from the HBO Original Series, Volume 4*.

Another example of these creative collabs includes a cover of the iconic psychedelic track "Season of the Witch," by Scottish singer-songwriter, Donovan. For the *True Blood* adaptation, Donovan was joined by British singer-songwriter Karen Elson, whose debut album, *The Ghost Who Walks*, was produced by Jack White, her husband at the time. The duo's version of the song is the opening track on *True Blood: Music From The HBO Original Series Volume 3*, and was also featured as a B-side on Elson's album (Spotify, n.d.c.).

Perhaps most memorable of *True Blood* singles, Calamar brought together Neko Case and Nick Cave for the show's fourth season premiere. For the episode, titled "She's Not There," the writer reportedly planned for Santana's cover of The Zombies' original song. Calamar, however, opted to do something original and contacted the two iconic artists to collaborate for a fresh version. According to Calamar, Adcock arranged the instrumentals of the track, Case sang her part from a studio in Seattle, and Cave travelled to LA. to record with Calamar. Their reimagining of the '60s classic joined Elson's cover on *True Blood*'s Grammy-nominated soundtrack album.

Calamar's unique strategy provides *True Blood* with still more added benefits and marketing power than can be imagined by the world's largest marketing agencies. By bringing artists of different eras and with different audiences together to collaborate on a creative cover like "She's Not There," Calamar engages diverse fanbases and encourages discussion across multiple fronts. This attracts new interest in the show, especially with those of *True Blood*'s target demographic that have yet to watch the show. In this way, music is just as strong of a draw for new viewers as the plot itself.

"HBO and Alan Ball's main drive is just to do what's right for the show, and anything else is kind of an afterthought," said Calamar on *True Blood*'s soundtracks. "It was pretty much me that pushed to have these soundtrack albums out. They certainly didn't fight it too much, but that wasn't really part of their plan to release a soundtrack album, and me doing these new recordings and bringing in these artists. I won't say it was a nuisance to them, but it was an extra thing that they had to deal with that wasn't necessarily a big priority to them."

What wasn't a big priority to the studio and showrunner ended up being widely received by *True Blood*'s audience. Grammy nominations, monetized assets, increased consumer engagement – Gary Calamar's decision to repurpose the music helped elevate *True Blood* from just a TV show into an interactive brand.

A big reason why *True Blood*'s music was so successful was the artist partnerships that Gary cultivated – C.C. Adcock's involvement most notably. During our interview, Gary said that C.C. had written a theme song for *True Blood* and even offered to act in the show, if they wanted to leverage his genuine Louisiana character even further. While these did not transpire, C.C.'s influence on the authenticity of *True Blood*'s music truly shows the benefits that only a strong artist relationship can offer.

The strong sonic identity that Gary created for the show had some viewers, and me in particular, tuning in every week just to hear the song he would pick for the closing credits. Literally, I didn't miss one episode, and it wasn't because I was obsessed with the plot – I was waiting to discover the new songs or creations that Gary crafted. It gave DJs, tastemakers, and music-lovers something new to share and a weekly topic to discuss. This creates massive value for the viewer and promotes the show in an innovative, unexpected way. In online forums on the show, many viewers said they enjoyed watching *True Blood*, but that it was the music that they came for. There's no bigger nod to the art of marketing with music.

Power to the Indie Artist

(*with Jonathan Christiansen*)

We hear the stories of artists who wanted to make it so badly, they moved to LA and slept in their car, hustling every day until they got their big break. As supervisors are becoming the new rockstars, sometimes the hustle becomes just as intense. Now one of the most up-and-coming names on the scene, I love when Jonathan Christiansen tells his story of wanting nothing more in life than to become a music supervisor. He was so sure of his need to become a supervisor that in his very early 20s, he packed up his things, drove to LA and slept in his car, knowing that if he was persistent enough, someone would open the door. Hustlin' DJ gigs at night and knocking on supervisors' doors during the day, his wish was finally granted when the founders of Hit The Ground Running invited Jonathan in as an intern.

Now, as a music supervisor at Hit The Ground Running, an independent music supervision company that has worked on shows such as *Entourage* and *Silicon Valley*, Jonathan Christiansen has acquired credits on dozens of television shows and hundreds of episodes. On top of that, he's still one of the best DJs to rock a party.

One of Christiansen's recent projects is the Starz original program *Power*, a crime drama created and executive produced by 50 Cent. Chronicling the double life of James "Ghost" St. Patrick, owner of an up-and-coming New York club called Truth and participant in the city's underground network of drugs, *Power* takes full advantage of the marketing power of music. An elite nightclub, underground cultures, New York City, produced by multi-platinum hip-hop artist 50 Cent: music is certainly one of the main focal points of *Power*.

The characters and the story that *Power* portrays may be fictional, but the world of the show is as real as New York City's actual nightlife crowd. Chock full of social elites and underground moguls, everything about *Power* needed to be authentic and ahead of the curve in order to really draw the viewer in. This means the fashion, the slang, and especially the music.

For this reason, Christiansen – who DJs throughout the Los Angeles nightlife scene as MIXMASON – was tapped as music supervisor. The critical role music plays in the TV show also explains 50 Cent's role in *Power*.

According to Christiansen, 50's involvement had a strong influence on the show's sonic identity. While the show is reflective of the themes first introduced in his breakout album, *Get Rich or Die Tryin'*, *Power* features several songs from 50's 2014 album, *Animal Ambition*. Though *Get Rich or Die Tryin'* was extremely successful, Christiansen incorporated songs from 50's newer album to develop cross-promotional leverage between *Animal Ambition* and *Power* (Christiansen, 2014).

The music industry being very aware of how this correlation could drive album sales, the rapper's fifth studio album was released the same week as the premiere of *Power*, and a lot of the end credits for the show's first season were scored with his songs, including "Twisted," "Winners Circle," "Irregular Heartbeat," and "Animal Ambition." In this way, *Power* helped promote 50's new album and vice versa, a tactful strategy that reflects Christiansen's understanding of the marketing power of music.

Additionally, 50 created the theme song for the show, "Big Rich Town," which he released along with a music video two months before the show's launch to attract his fans to the show. Featuring R&B singer Joe, the video includes clips of Ghost living his double life (Cent, n.d.).

The parallels can hardly be considered coincidental. Cross-promotion with 50's album, licensing several of his tracks in the end credits, and even basing the plot partly on the rapper's life – it is evident that *Power* would be a completely different show if it wasn't for the artist partnership with 50 Cent.

"Aside from that, 50 was very involved with the overall sound of the show and would definitely weigh in where he felt inclined," said Christiansen. "[For example], 50 [and] other execs on the show wanted [Ghost's] club to sound ultra-contemporary, exactly as if a brand-new club actually was opening in New York and was looking to appeal to New York's young, fashionable elite."

It was Christiansen's job to not just place songs that fit the scene, but to license music that's currently buzzing. This adds to the marketing of the show, as it creates new ways for consumers to engage with and talk about *Power*, extending the buzz beyond the 60-minute airtime.

The music at Truth, *Power*'s fictional club that caters to New York's most prominent players, emerged from the collaborative curation of the show's music team. Music supervision, as Christiansen put it, is certainly a team effort. For his part, Christiansen seeks to use the work of emerging, independent artists as frequently as possible, the music supervisor said, because "licensing real artists in as many spots as physically possible gives authenticity to that piece of the show."

The creators of *Power* crafted Truth into a club that truly felt real, and filled it with actual industry influencers and New York socialites. No showrunner worth his or her salt would take such creative strides only to license lame production music to play in the background. To do so would tarnish the sense of realism that the show had cultivated so meticulously. Using cool, authentic music is just as important as every other aspect of putting a show together, especially for *Power*.

To build that authenticity for Truth, Christiansen said he partly pulled from his personal experiences of DJ'ing throughout Los Angeles' nightlife scene, performing at red carpet premieres and as a resident artist in LA's hottest clubs. In addition to minding what songs to license in the club, Christiansen built Truth into a true NYC club by featuring on-screen appearances by some of the city's most talented DJs and artists, such as Just Blaze, Nina Sky, Branchez, DJ Envy, and other New York staples.

When millions of viewers can see these artists in an environment like Truth, they hear the music as if it was truly mixed for the club, and might then become fans. These syncs are especially helpful for viewers, because they would otherwise have to sort blindly through the vast heap of emerging artists populating the industry today to find the kind of music featured in *Power*.

Many people suggest that this oversaturation of new artists makes it harder than ever to get noticed. Christiansen, however, indicated that oversaturation may be an indirect benefit to artists. When more artists have widespread access to high-quality recording equipment, it drives a lower price-point in the marketplace, Christiansen explained. And though this surplus might result in lower up-front pay for artists, they're ultimately licensed more often in place of stock music because supervisors can now afford them.

"The cost savings that you get from using a stock production library might be relatively negligible when compared to licensing an independent musician," continued Christiansen. "Funding them directly with money to continue their craft, whether that be recording, mixing, mastering, touring, buying a van to go on a tour, or whatever it may be. So as a music supervisor, I will always support that."

Using cool, real artists that are on the rise in New York helps the audience discover new music, a takeaway they can count on the show to deliver on a consistent basis. Christiansen is digging through tens of thousands of rising New York artists and picking the ones he believes are best. He's doing the heavy lifting so the audience can look to *Power* to be a trusted filter of the best new music on the scene. They instinctively share that music with their peers, which gets consumers talking about the show in a very organic way. This is a great example of the marketing power of music and its limitless potential to attract, immerse, and extend the relationship with the viewers.

On-screen appearances like *Power*'s featured DJs and artists initiate the engagement process between the show, the artist, and the viewer – an engagement process that typically ends with the episode's credits unless shows proactively leverage their ancillary touchpoints to keep the engagement cycle running.

"It's a logical, easy way for a network/show to increase viewer engagement throughout the week, beyond just the 30–60 minutes their show is airing," said Christiansen. "If someone Shazams [the song], and it's on Spotify or on SoundCloud, that's a real crossover, that's a real opportunity to engage a viewer and create a potential real-life fan."

For *Power* and for the rest of their shows, Christiansen and Hit The Ground Running list all of the shows they work with on their website and provide a Spotify playlist for each. These playlists share each song licensed for the shows' most recently aired episodes.

"The Spotify playlists also help highlight some of the indie or lesser-known artists that we're syncing, in addition to the major or mainstream artists," said Christiansen. "It also creates a social aspect [...]. We update them weekly, so anyone who follows the playlist can see the week's worth of music."

One of the songs on the Power playlist is "V.I.P." by Play. *Power* worked with the Brooklyn-based hip-hop artist and his label, Pink Kiss Entertainment, to feature the song before its official release. In the last scene of the season's final episode, "V.I.P." bumps its poppy bass line as gunfire fills club Truth. Viewers immediately flocked to sites like TuneFind and frantically asked each other for the title of the song, at which point a familiar-looking name would chime in and ease the tension.

"Play 'V.I.P.,'" TuneFind user @MIXMASON shared, but followed up with a disappointing reply. "It's just not released yet." Users posted links to Play's Facebook and iTunes pages where fans could pre-order the track. Two weeks after its premiere on *Power*'s season finale, the emerging artist's debut single finally dropped and Christiansen added it to *Power*'s Spotify playlist immediately (TuneFind, n.d.).

"I think the greatest thing about Spotify [...] is the ability to dive into back catalog," said Christiansen. "As soon as you hear one song, it's not a trip to the record store in a few weeks when you have the time and money to invest in it. It's right away. You can go back, go 'Wow I love this artist,' and you can become a fan of the artists so quickly because it's right at your fingertips. [It's] that discovery factor."

Jonathan Christiansen demonstrates how closely a music supervisor can work with their ancillary touchpoints to push attention to both the artists and the TV show. His anonymous presence in the TuneFind message boards is hugely reflective of this effort. Jonathan took his music strategy deep into the social site, directly interacted with *Power* viewers, and connected them with Play. And all of this occurred outside of any official Starz or *Power* website.

Jonathan's above-and-beyond efforts show the extent that today's music supervisor is willing to go to further foster engagement with fans and deepen the connection between the show, the artist, and the consumer. Because of his success, Jonathan's actions will likely become a trend that networks, studios, and shows will come to expect of music supervisors as well as something the music industry will start asking for more often. It demonstrates the incredible difference that not only using the right song makes, but also the strong marketing power of music when it is used to connect with the viewers beyond the 30- or 60-minute show.

The Vampire Diaries and Music for Millennials

(*with Chris Mollere*)

Founder of full-service firm Fusion Music Supervision, Chris Mollere has earned credits on over 25 projects, including over 100 episodes of *Pretty Little Liars*. His Hollywood experience began as a producer's/composer's assistant at Music Forever, where he served as a liaison with record labels, directors, and producers. It was there that he first worked in music supervision, on the film, *Memory*.

Since that first project, Mollere's name has gone almost as viral as the songs he chooses. A big part of this notoriety has come from his work on the CW series, *The Vampire Diaries*, and its spinoff, *The Originals*.

Though watched by consumers of all ages, *The Vampire Diaries* has a mostly young audience of teenaged and young adult viewers – a demographic very connected to trends in the music space. Accordingly, the sonic identity of the show often includes licensing artists who have yet to fully break into a household name. Young people of all demographics and backgrounds place a great amount of value in music discovery. In an August 2014 study by research brand Voxburner, the company's head of insights, Luke Mitchell, asserted

that, "music remains an important interest among young people and at a time of discovery, identity development, and high social activity, it can be defining" (Macleod, 2014).

To fully captivate his viewers and increase immersion, Mollere bases a lot of his music strategy on giving viewers what they want from any good music curator: songs they haven't heard before.

"More and more people are actually going out there and seeking out new music, and they want to be the ones to find it first," said Mollere. "Whether that's from a TV show, a song list, or they hear a song on that spot, then that's their new favorite song. [...] People get satisfaction in finding music, and I'm happy for people who claim to find it" (Mollere, Music Supervisor, 2014).

In episode 6:15 of *The Vampire Diaries*, Mollere licensed the song "Shine" by Night Terrors of 1927, an indie-pop duo who released their debut album, *Everything's Coming Up Roses*, only weeks prior through Atlantic. For many viewers, this was likely their first time hearing the song. As something new, young, and exciting, this sync perfectly reflects the sonic identity of *The Vampire Diaries*. It also speaks to Mollere's goal as the show's music supervisor: cater to the consumers, support indie artists, and elevate the content of the show.

cater to the consumers, support indie artists, and elevate the content of the show

"You have to look at [music] from the perception of the show and also the audience," said Mollere. "You have to kind of go outside your own body and your own mind to find music that's not necessarily what you think is good, but what's proper in the show and for the fanbase. So you have to look at it in different ways, but in addition to that, it's trying to get in the head of the show. It's trying to find ways to navigate musically, to create that vision and to fulfill that vision musically for each episode – just to find the music identity."

According to The CW's website, *The Vampire Diaries* typically licenses between five and ten songs each episode (CW TV, n.d.). Most of those songs are like "Shine": indie tracks from up-and-coming artists that viewers may have never heard before.

For the final scene of the show's season three finale in 2012, Mollere selected a song that no one – no matter how in tune to the music industry they were – had ever heard before.

"We premiered a new Sigur Ros track from their last record on *The Vampire Diaries* two weeks before the record came out," said Mollere. "I talked them into doing it, but once they did, they started advertising for it and there were people that actually watched the show because the band was having a song premiere on *The Vampire Diaries*, because it couldn't be heard anywhere else."

The song was "Dauðalogn" (meaning "Dead Calm" in English), a six-minute track featuring the U.K. choir, The Sixteen. One of eight tracks on the band's sixth studio album, *Valtari*, the song was synced for a big, four-minute placement in that season finale of *The Vampire Diaries*. The final scene was ripe with underwater heartache and vampiric drama, the emotional power of which was heightened by Mollere's selection of "Dauðalogn." Sigur Ros followers, post-rock devotees, and music bloggers alike flocked to the show to watch that scene, joining the mass of *TVD* fans who had already learned to listen for Mollere's music curation to find new bands each episode. As well, Mollere's strong musical strategy demonstrates how music can become the primary engagement factor, sending new viewers who have managed to avoid typical marketing including ads, promos, and word of mouth, to engage with the show.

"Artists will tell us that people go to shows and fans will [say], 'Dude, I heard about you from *Vampire Diaries*, you had a song on there,' and things like that," said Mollere. "It's cool to make it more intriguing for artists to feature their music. They're already kind enough to let us feature their music, so anything else we can do to help them further their career and help them out, we're happy to do."

This is how viewers discover new artists and how music fans discover TV shows: it all begins with a sync. However, the primary touchpoint alone won't always convert viewers to fans.

"The dangerous part about putting music in television shows and films is that we basically live in an era where there's so much information going on," said Mollere. "So, if people don't have the information that they want immediately, they forget about it."

Anyone familiar with Mollere can likely attest to his devotion to connecting his television audience with their recently discovered artists. The music supervisor developed a relationship with mobile music app Shazam and works with them to ensure each of the songs placed in his shows are uploaded, tagged, and easily discoverable. Additionally, immediately after each airing of *The Vampire Diaries* and *The Originals*, Mollere posts on Twitter the names of every song and artist licensed during the episode (Mollere, *@cmollere*, n.d.).

"It gets people excited about [the music]. They can have the information that they want to know right away, so they can go buy it," said Mollere. "If we miss out on that, then the artists are missing out, and if we don't support the artists, then we won't have music to place. Artists [would] have to go and get jobs because they can't focus on music, and from there we're all going to be hurting."

The power of immediate discovery is substantial, as demonstrated by Shazam. According to the media engagement company in 2013, its services generated $300 million in music download sales annually and were responsible for one in every fourteen downloads (Resnikoff, 2013). Reflective of Shazam's influence, Mollere's social media effort has yielded evident success, too. Every post is typically retweeted and favorited fifty times each, and his following consists of 18.5 thousand, more substantial than the average supervisor. These numbers show how powerfully engaging music can be, as well as the power of ancillary touchpoints like social media when applied to music strategy and marketing efforts.

Chris Mollere offers us a powerful idea: supporting your artist community is an investment in your own project. Whether that's featuring a song from a newly released album, collaborating with an artist for a mutually beneficial sync, or cross-promoting via social media – there's a lot a TV show can do to help the artists whose music they license.

The Vampire Diaries shows how well that practice can pay off for a show. Chris was able to increase engagement with the show's audience, as well as attract many new viewers to the show – all through creative music supervision. So successful was *The Vampire Diaries*, the CW launched its spinoff, *The Originals*, four years after *TVD* premiered. While music was not the primary reason for the launch of the new show, the strong consumer engagement caused in part by Chris's music strategy was certainly a contribution.

chapter 6

Film

Remember the days when everyone bought the soundtrack to a movie? Well, unlike everything else that used to be great in the music industry and has died, soundtracks continue to hold a formidable role in the lives of consumers. In fact, two of the top 10 selling albums last year were soundtracks (IFPI, 2015). Unlike TV, in which we tune in weekly to discover music and the TV shows are our weekly curators of music discovery, when music strategy is executed correctly in movies the soundtrack extends the experience and returns us to that story from which we first heard it. Such is the power of both passion points – story and music.

Two of the top 10 selling albums last year were soundtracks

People might ask the modern consumer why she spends so much money on movies, and on entertainment in general. Well, because life is not so easy. Sometimes, it just plain sucks and we need an escape, a distraction, or even just a reminder of how great life can be. This is one reason why story is such a perennial passion point for humankind. Story, in part, justifies some of the BS that we deal with as naturally suffering people. Story explains and, depending on your own taste, represents a part of you that you could otherwise not rationalize or put into words.

Personally, I hate scary movies. From when I was little until now they have always been traumatizing experiences for me. After watching a horror movie, I can't sleep for a week. Scary movies and ghost stories have ruined my love of hiking in the wilderness, swimming in lagoons, and exploring old, abandoned barns. So, tell me why I spent a year of my life only watching horror movies? Well, because I had a job that sucked and I was miserable all day. I was so stressed and upset when I'd come home from work that the only thing that would distract me from my own waking nightmare was a horror movie. I would have preferred to not be able to sleep because I was afraid of ghosts rather than be awake all night dreading another day of work in the morning. I hated scary movies, but I needed their powers of transportation in order to escape to a different world. That's what movies, and story in general, do for us. Usually, we like to be taken to a happier place; however, sometimes we need the things that make a bad day at work seem like a better situation than we imagine possible to what it'd be like if we were locked in a basement with murderous clowns.

So, how does all of this translate to movie soundtrack sales? Because music is the emotional connection to the viewer. That's the bridge between reality and surreality. The nostalgic properties inherent in music, as well as the emotional influence that the marriage of story and music has over the hearts of audiences, can transform the perspective of life as few other experiences can. It's what makes us feel as if we've been truly transported to a different world.

Non-diegetic music also provides the context for the scene – it's an emotional cue that precedes suspense. Imagine these scenes.

A couple is walking hand-in-hand through an idyllic countryside. Their stroll through a sun-kissed meadow is painted gold by the autumnal sunset and, as the camera follows behind them, you see them turn their heads towards each other and smile almost imperceptibly. While this would undoubtedly seem like a pleasant scene in a lighthearted RomCom, a slow, baritone organ that pulses behind them, growing ever faster as the camera gets closer to the couple, alerts the viewer that this date is about to come to an abrupt end.

Similarly, in another scene, a young woman is wading in open water, sunlight dappling the water and gilding her blonde hair with its shine. She's smiling, even laughing as she splashes her lithe arms against the surface of the water. Once again, what would seem like a pleasant scene darkens when the now iconic music kicks in. Daa... na. Da..na. Da.na. Da-na-da-na-da-na-da-na. Since then, the *Jaws* music became one of the poster songs for non-diegetic music and its effect on the viewing experience – and that emotion sticks with us for the rest of our lives and (unfortunately for me) can be triggered anytime afterwards when we hear that music again.

For the same reason that the music of *Jaws* became representative of dread, the music of *Frozen* has become symbolic of joy for an entire generation. When children are in the backseat of their parents' car, bickering about the placement of each other's feet on the floor mat, the soundtrack immediately lulls them back to the enchanting world of *Frozen*. In a similar, though grimmer vein, whenever my brother starts humming the *Jaws* theme after I've dived into the ocean, I am literally terrified and my jolly frolicking time is genuinely ruined.

The soundtrack is the way to extend the movie experience. It maintains a tether to the story and emotions of the film, and an access point to the world long after you leave the theater. Though that world may be one which you feel so immersed in while watching, few (if any) consumers could watch that same film every day; however, the soundtrack to that film could run on repeat for months and will retain its charm. I know of at least one person – Zach Miller, the Associate Editor to this book, in fact – who listens to the entire soundtrack to *Les Misérables* every day in his life, and genuine tears always stain his face throughout the experience every time.

The formula for successful music supervision in film follows the same principles as television, video games, and even advertising; however, the tactics are entirely different. In fact, music supervisors can avail themselves to the same ten touchpoints in film and television to achieve the same three results of music strategy; however, they will create an entirely different process for success, as the following interviews demonstrate. These touchpoints, once again, are:

1. Sonic Identity
2. Promos/Trailers
3. Title Sequence/Theme Songs
4. Non-Diegetic Syncs
5. Diegetic Syncs
6. Social Media
7. Web Pages
8. Artist Relationships
9. Monetizable Assets
10. Live Activations

The *James Bond 007* franchise has created a sonic identity that will endure for many years to come, and because of its timeless status, music supervisors and producers can experiment with creative licensing to enhance the music experience for viewers. For example, the latest *Bond* flick, following the franchise's music strategy since the first *007* film, partnered with popular artist Adele to create a custom song for the film that went on to have an entire life of its own in the hearts and playlists of consumers. In another example, Ed Sheeran wrote an original song for one of 2014's hottest films, *The Fault in Our Stars*. Although not used in the official trailer, the music that was used to advertise and attract viewers shared the same sonic identity based on Sheeran's song, "All of the Stars," that helped shape the sound of the film. The music video was released one month before the movie, which directed all of Sheeran's fans to theaters to see the movie that had so intimately tied music into its experience. It was then released as the first song on the soundtrack, further extending the relationship beyond the theaters.

Artist partnerships such as these illustrate how the marketing power of music in film and all media is resurrecting the industry. The more labels, managers, and artists coordinate with the movie's release, the more benefit they will receive, too. Cross-promotional opportunities are boundless, especially when music is interwoven with the plot to such a degree that an onscreen artist performance is warranted – the most authentic example of diegetic music. For the film, it accesses an entirely new fanbase, as the artist will undoubtedly promote the film doubly if they appear in it as themselves. For the artist, it provides a platform to perform before an entirely new audience in an engaging medium. And for viewers, it authenticates the story and immerses them even more into the film.

Trailer Music

Movie trailers are a prominent component of the film industry – for movies, it is the premier representation of the attraction function of music strategy. Before seeing a film, consumers almost always see a trailer to instigate that desire. In order to sell a film, you need to sell the trailer. And in order to sell the trailer, you need killer music.

In order to sell a film, you need to sell the trailer

For Sanaz Lavaedian, harnessing the marketing power of music for film trailers is nearly second nature.

According to Sanaz, who currently heads the music department for entertainment creative agency mOcean, she first truly noticed music in film when she was 9 years old and watching *Pulp Fiction*, during the scene in which the characters Vince and Mia go to the Wallace household, and the Urge Overkill cover of "Girl, You'll Be a Woman Soon" begins to play. Ever since then, Sanaz says, music supervision was something she was always subconsciously interested in before even knowing it was a career choice.

"I remember that was the first 'Aha!' moment where I noticed the effect the music had on me. From there I always paid attention to music in film and, later, music in TV," she said. "I started doing research on it in high school, because I remember watching *The Virgin Suicides*, which was the second film that really blew my mind in terms of the music usage. It's definitely still one of my favorite movies in terms of music supervision. I started researching it and discovered that music supervision is a real career choice. So I always kept it in the back of my head" (Lavaedian, 2015).

From there, Sanaz attended UCLA and intended to then go to law school; however, after some contemplative soul searching, Sanaz said she discovered that music supervision was her true passion, and she decided to pursue it.

"I gave myself a year and a half to see if anything would come of it. So when I graduated UCLA, I quit my full-time job and just started looking for internships, cold calling different music supervisors and telling them that I was interested and would work for free. Luckily, Robin Kaye, the music supervisor for *American Idol*, hired me on. I started as a music clearance coordinator for *The Singing Bee* and she taught me how to fill out requests and do licenses on the publishing side."

For most students and graduates interested in music supervision, internships are the foremost entry point into the industry. A craft that first relies on a foundation of publishing, licensing, and rights negotiation, finding a mentor to train those preeminent skills is pivotal before leaping into a full-scale project on one's own. From there, Sanaz worked with notable supervisor Robin Urdang, where she not only worked clearance and publishing on master rights, but was also involved with creative – probably the most alluring aspect of the job. Her early credits including the television shows *Burn Notice*, *Brothers and Sisters*, and *The Good Guys*, as well as the films *Beginners*, *Rabbit Hole*, *The Oranges*, and *Piranha 3D*.

Sanaz reportedly knew the music supervisor at mOcean through mutual friends and was hired on as music coordinator, where she first began working with trailers. Four-and-a-half years later, Sanaz rose to run the music department and has become an expert on the subject, despite the vast differences in mediums between TV, films, and trailers.

"When it comes to film and TV, you have the entire duration of the film or the episode to come up with a musical direction," Sanaz explained. "With trailers, it's so different because we only have a minute to two-and-a-half minutes to come up with a musical direction and pique interest in an audience to come see a movie."

"We're technically marketing and a trailer is technically a commercial. We don't have an hour-long episode to choose all these different songs to set the mood or musical direction."

Another massive difference between trailers and the film and TV industries is that the latter are not exclusive, which means that a marketing department at a studio can hire two to three different trailer houses to work on the same project, Sanaz said. Whichever house the studio likes best ends up winning, and frustratingly, trailers that had been in development for up to a year may never see the light of day.

Additionally, timelines for trailers are vastly different. Often, Sanaz and the mOcean team will begin working on a trailer when the film goes into production and receive the dailies, yet at other times they will get a fully assembled film and have to cut a trailer in two days. Furthermore, budgets are incredibly different. Because trailers are considered marketing, which often have much greater music budgets, some trailer music budgets can be significantly more than the music budget of the actual film.

"With film or a TV show, you have to be very budget conscious," Sanaz said. "Say you're working on a TV show and you have a [certain] budget for that episode, you might be using twenty songs, so you have to budget accordingly. When it comes to a trailer, when I pitch music, I'm oftentimes not even thinking about the budget. If the studio likes the song enough, they'll pay for it. The ability to choose songs without being restricted by a budget is really freeing for me."

Additionally, trailer music undergoes an entirely different approval process than music in film, beginning with the filmmaker or the head of marketing for a studio, for example. At mOcean, Sanaz will curate a folder of music she thinks suits the project, which her editor and producer listen to. If they like something, they'll start cutting with it, she says. Then once the whole trailer is cut with the song, the client at the studio is presented with it. If they like it, they'll show the filmmaker, and if the filmmaker likes it, they'll show it to the head of marketing at the studio. Finally, if they like it, the trailer will go to test in a focus group.

"Everyone has to be on board with the music for the approval process to finish," Sanaz said. "If one person along the way doesn't like it, then it's back to square one and we start from scratch."

This could be a frustrating thing for the supervisor as well as the music industry. If an artist or label knows their song is being pitched for a trailer, it's the type of placement that can make or break their career. But it's the supervisor's job to never settle, as the impact of a trailer could lead to a movie's box office success, or lack thereof.

"Music in trailers is so important, because we're trying to evoke a certain emotion while you're watching it," Sanaz explained. "I work based on how something makes me feel, which is how I pitch it for trailers."

"You want a trailer to be memorable. If someone watches a trailer at the beginning of the film, you want them to leave the theater at the end of the film still thinking about it. Whether it's because they recognize the song, and they love it, so now they're thinking about the trailer, or whether they're just blown away by this new piece of music that made them feel something and resonated with them. That, to me, is a huge win personally, because that's what music supervision has done for me. It's moments like that which have inspired me to do what I do. So for me to be able to create that for other people is so gratifying, but also from a business aspect, that's what you want because you want people to think about the trailer and the film so that they go watch it."

It's hard to imagine that picking one song to promote a movie could have an impact on a 100+ million-dollar film with massively recognized actors, but where music is usually the first budget to get cut in a production, the studios recognize the marketing importance of music enough in trailers that it's the one time that they open their pocketbooks for a song.

As fun as it might sound to pick music for trailers, Sanaz has to take her job very seriously because as she says, "Music can make or break a trailer, which, in turn, can make or break a film."

Music That Attracts

As these case studies hopefully illustrate, everyone gets into the industry differently, and there's no right or wrong way to go about it. From sleeping in your car and knocking on doors like Christiansen, to cold-calling like Sanaz, or moving from the legal department like Ann Kline, Kier Lehman's path to music supervision is perhaps the most conventional, though even his journey was marked by surprises.

Kier originally studied Music for Media in college, focusing on writing and producing music for media such as film scoring and commercial jingles, which was, Kier said, his first introduction to how music and picture work together. Upon graduation, Kier moved back to Los Angeles and was introduced to a music supervisor, who offered Kier an internship. Kier ended up working for that supervisor for five years and, after paying his dues as an assistant doing research for licensing, drafting, quote requests, and other related tasks, eventually started pitching creative ideas to his boss. After he was there for a few years, Kier said he felt that he had learned enough to work independently as a music supervisor, which he did successfully (Lehman, 2015). About a year after going independent, he was offered a job at Sony Pictures as creative and the in-house executive music supervisor for their film department. That gave him the amazing opportunity to work on a range of different films of different genres and with all types of different budget levels.

It was while he was at Sony that I first met Kier, and he gave me our first-ever film placement, which was for the animated film, *Cloudy with a Chance of Meatballs*. After four years and learning all he could, Kier returned to independent music supervision, armed with more experience than ever.

At Sony, not only did Kier work as a music supervisor, but he was also charged with hiring music supervisors on films. As many people reading this book might be aspiring supervisors themselves, we took the opportunity to talk with Kier about what he looks for when hiring a supervisor and the skills, both personal and professional, required for the job.

"Aside from obvious knowledge of music, the music industry, and business, it seems from what I've learned that relationships with people, having people like to hang out with you, and being organized and attentive to detail are super important things that make a good supervisor."

Being a supervisor, you have to deal with many different people along the workflow, all with distinctive personalities. From executives at studios, to directors, actors, labels, and musicians, you have to be able to speak their language and vibe well with all of them, ensuring them you have their backs and best intentions at heart.

Another quality of Kier's unique to his path is having the academic background of a musician and producer, which allowed him to understand the production process of deciding how to pair sound and picture. As the liaison between the music and media worlds, music supervisors must know the vocabulary of each industry to ensure quality results in licensing a world-famous song all the way to commissioning a quality custom recording that suits the story.

"Being able to communicate and understand what a producer wants and being able to explain that to a composer or songwriter so we get to realize the producer or the director's vision in the best way possible," Kier said, is a pivotal role of the supervisor.

"As far as choosing songs versus writing songs, they're both very creative," Kier continued, discussing the difference between music supervision and composition. "I've always had a voracious appetite for new music and have always been searching in catalogs or for new things on the internet or in magazines or in record stores, so I always had a large knowledge of different styles. I used that creativity to pull from different genres or from different styles of music that could work for a project that may not be the initial thing that you would think about, or what the director or the writers have asked for."

This creative understanding of music, as well as his ability to socialize with people in tiny dark rooms or hang with people in crowded music venues, led Kier to play a prominent role in the popular film,

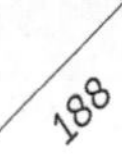

22 Jump Street, from which one scene in particular stood out for many viewers – the Spring Break scene when the popular artist Diplo is DJ'ing on screen.

"I remember it fondly," began Kier. "That was a tough spot because we shot with Diplo on set, so in a way we committed to having something that either was his music, something he was involved in, or something he approved of or cosigned. We were hoping that he might have something new and original we could have or if we could use one of his existing songs, which we already knew that we liked for the scene and the movie in general."

"So we shot the scene and on set he played a lot of different songs from his DJ sets and the crowd loved it. All the extras on set loved having him there, and it gave the vibe on the set a great, really high energy, because all the extras were so excited that he was DJ'ing from his set. So they were dancing and excited that they got a private Diplo show."

Watch the scene again and you'll feel the authentic excitement of the crowd. Like in a real Spring Break moment, the extras push towards the stage, throw their hands towards the DJ, and scream at the recognizable bass drops and mixes. This authenticity could not be manufactured – it was an organic result of having a real artist on set, opposed to hiring an actor to portray a DJ.

When the creators wrote the script, Kier said they imagined that the characters would go to a giant Spring Break party with an on-set music performance. In the script, they had originally written Bruno Mars to cast as the performance; however, the budget for Bruno Mars and his full band to star and perform on camera, as well as fly the entire act in and accommodate them with hotel rooms, did not fit into the budget, Kier said. So, he began to brainstorm music solutions.

"In the music world right now, DJs are incredibly popular," Kier said. "Kids are going to festivals and shows and clubs where the DJ is spinning with thousands of kids, lights, all this great club design and amazing sound systems. It seemed like authentically having a DJ be at this party made the most sense."

"I pitched them a few DJ ideas and Diplo was always my favorite pick, because I felt that he was not only authentic as being a DJ who was super popular, but he also had this kind of personality that goes beyond the music. He's got this crazy social media following, he's got these other musical projects like Major Lazer and the record label Mad Decent, so there were a lot of angles that I thought could help with the movie where we could maybe have access to his music and his label's music, which is music I was going to be pitching for the movie anyway."

"So, it just made sense to get him on camera, work with his label to get music, and have a personality that people would recognize instantly that felt authentic to the crowd in the movie and the audience of the movie. It seemed that he hit all the boxes of that," Kier said.

Kier said he and Diplo talked on set about his new music that he had, or if he had ideas that he wanted Kier to hear, at which point Diplo sent Kier "Too Turnt Up" by Flosstradamus and Waka Flocka Flame.

"When I tried it with the picture, I thought it was amazing. It had this really great build and it had this huge drop and it had the vocals from Waka Flocka, which were really high energy and really spoke to what was going on in the scene, which was people getting turnt up," said Kier. "The scene ended up needing a more high-stakes vibe to it, so we went through a few other songs and nothing was quite right. I went back to ["Too Turnt Up"], put it on the scene and played it again and felt that this was it. I felt it from the beginning but now that we knew better what the tone of the scene is, this is really the song."

Enlisting Diplo provided Kier and the film with a slew of benefits, all of which fall into music strategy and along the ten touchpoints of music in television. Diplo's sound matched, defined, and heightened the sonic identity of the scene. By featuring him in the official trailer, Diplo's underground, renowned personality attracted an entire generation of young people to take interest in the movie and show up at the box office. The diegetic use of his music, performance, and persona immersed viewers into the Spring Break scene and authenticated the story. Furthermore, forming that artist relationship opened possibilities for social media extension beyond the film for marketing and cross-promotion with Diplo.

Diplo has a built-in audience, from his social media followers and his fans, which is an entire audience of people that may or may not have been already interested in the movie. When they saw that Diplo would be involved, the movie studio could excite people already interested in the movie as well as those who are Diplo fans who may not have been aware of the film. According to Kier, the film tracked tons of social media conversations that were about Diplo's involvement in the film. Furthermore, Diplo posted Instagram pictures of the set, Tweeted about the release, and cross-promoted his music and the film to his audience.

"It just kind of adds a specific reach to the overall marketing of the movie. They obviously want to connect with as many people as possible, but if you could connect with specific groups that are already probably interested or will be interested because they're a fan of that person, then it makes that marketing much stronger and the likelihood that those people are going to go see that movie even stronger," said Kier.

To even further heighten the marketing power of music and Diplo's involvement with the film, Flosstradamus waited for the release of *22 Jump Street* in June 2014 to officially release the song, "Too Turnt Up." By timing the releases, working together with the music industry to ensure the greatest possible impact for both the music and the film, Kier ensured that the consumer experience – before, during, and after the film – was as attractive, immersive, and extensive as possible.

By understanding the emotional capabilities of music in the hearts of consumers, he transformed *22 Jump Street* from a 120-minute film into a multisensory story that could be experienced many ways, including through music. On top of bringing maximum value to the film, Kier's expert understanding of how to integrate music effectively brought amazing value back to the music industry.

"With so many artists out there and so much music out there, people are having a hard time weeding through all of it," Kier said. "Having a placement in a TV show or a movie brings a different kind of connection to a piece of music than if you just heard it on the radio, because you've got this emotional storyline going on and this piece of music that's connected and attached to that storyline to heighten the emotion. I think it works both ways in enhancing the show, but also bringing another connection to the song that you might not have had if you just heard it on its own."

"For me, when I see a great piece of music used with a great picture, I always will keep that connection to the song and it will remind me of the scene, the first time I heard it or the millionth time I heard it. But it was used so well in a great scene that it will add to my relationship with that song going forward. I think that it's gone up and down in what the perceived value [of music in film] is, but right now it's a pretty strong value."

For *22 Jump Street*, that value of music was heightened due to Kier's expert employment of music strategy into the project. First, Kier and the creators of the film had to determine the sonic identity of the film. As the film is meant to simulate a college experience, that meant music would have to play a strong role in the project – college students (as most readers of this book can probably attest) define themselves through music. It's a form of social identification, as well as communication. As the audience for *22 Jump Street* was also predominantly college-aged consumers, authenticity was also supremely important. Viewers would know immediately if the music personality was inauthentic, which would render the entire film inauthentic and thus obliterate the central function of music in film: immersion.

By featuring "Too Turnt Up" in the pivotal Spring Break scene, viewers were wholly immersed into the story. The song itself perfectly defined the moment, and as it was released in tandem to the film, that scene was undoubtedly many viewers' first time hearing it. As Kier noted, a great sync sticks with most viewers. For many fans of *22 Jump Street*, the ecstatic emotions that are definitive of a bombastic Spring Break party are undoubtedly recalled whenever they hear the Flosstradamus track now. Whether they know it or not, this recall is surely correlated to their ingrained memories of experiencing that song with the film. Furthermore, Diplo's onscreen performance excited more than a handful of viewers, as the social media conversations illustrate. In the same way that the on-set extras were genuinely excited for a real, live performance by the notorious DJ, moviegoers experienced a similar rush that hits us all when our favorite artist walks on stage after soundcheck at a concert.

Music in *22 Jump Street* did far more than simply support the content, as is often described to be the core function of music in media. Not only did Kier's music supervision support the picture, but it became a vehicle for story in itself, constantly communicating with viewers, sometimes subconsciously and sometimes directly, in order to maintain their captive attention. The music transformed them from passive viewers into an active audience, one whose energy was always high despite exerting no more physical activity than scooping popcorn from a bucket.

The music transformed them from passive viewers into an active audience

That's the emotional power of music, a sensation all of us are familiar with. The marketing power of music is knowing how to unleash the full range of music in media, wherein one can use music to both support the content and provide an authentic, engaging musical experience.

Music That Immerses

As music supervisor Sarah Webster remembers it, the day she decided she wanted to be a music supervisor was a beautiful June day and the last day of eighth grade, with the windows cast open. The class had read the book *The Outsiders* and their teacher had rewarded them with a viewing of the film to wrap up the school year. Sarah sat in the front row, her head clasped in her hands, as her eyes and ears were captivated most especially by the end credits song, an original by Stevie Wonder that he had written specifically for the film.

"I was so captured by this piece of music," Sarah recalls. "I was so moved by the music that I wondered, who is in charge of choosing music for movies? How does this happen? What is the process? How do I get into this? That stayed with me for a very long time. Fifteen years later I got my first gig as a music supervisor and I got to choose the end credits song."

"Honestly, it was my love of music," Sarah said on how she got her foot in the door of the music supervision industry. "People always say follow what you're passionate about and a career will follow. For me that was very true. I was entirely immersed in the dance music culture that was thriving on the West Coast – deep house music in the early '90s. It was by virtue of my knowing everyone just from being part of the community – the record labels, the publishing companies, the DJs."

From that background, Sarah was tapped by some friends to work for their software development company as they needed music licensed for a product they were building for a video game console. They knew that Sarah had already built a lot of strong relationships in the industry. Their lawyer taught Sarah the legalese of music licensing, which gave her a springboard to then work for two premier House music record labels, Naked Music and Satellite Records. Back in Vancouver, she found a company with a department in Film Music, pitched them her services, and was hired on the spot as a music supervisor, hardly fifteen years after her first desire to break into the industry after that fateful June day.

"Film is a wonderful vehicle because we can do so many things with the music," Sarah said. "We can break emerging artists that people perhaps haven't heard of before, we can resurrect songs from the '80s that people haven't heard in a loud sound system that movie theaters provide, and we can have artists writing. It's just an amazing vehicle."

This perspective of music in film is a shared vision among the industry's leading music supervisors, though it hasn't yet fully permeated the film industry as a whole: seeing film as a vehicle for more than solely the picture. As the Social Empowerment theory postulates, consumers want their lives enriched by all content experiences, and they want the value of that experience to be as powerful as possible. First and foremost, great film requires great storytelling. This is the key passion point that is satisfied by the film industry. However, movies have the capability of providing so much more value to the human experience in addition to a powerful story. Additionally, consumers have the power to choose those films that do go the extra mile and provide something of greater value, meaning the studios that don't consider Social Empowerment with their films will gradually lose more and more moviegoers.

There are numerous examples of ways that the film industry can provide for these consumer passion points. Examples include the pioneering films that also incorporate conversations on social issues, which creates a greater dialogue with consumers that lives beyond the script. In other examples, passion points like fashion or sports are reflected when films can both respond to consumer interests and engage viewers with strong story. It is probably impossible to fulfill every consumer passion point with one film. Filmmakers must therefore consider their target audience and determine which passion points best suit the story of the film. Fortunately for them, music is the most shared passion point among consumers, making music an obvious vehicle for engagement that every project should incorporate, especially as all films feature music anyway. The differentiating factor requires filmmakers to consider music as a path to consumer engagement and not simply a support beam for their story. Music can do both, and savvy supervisors like Sarah are championing this theory and subsequently are changing the landscape of music in film one sync at a time.

"There's nothing like music to evoke emotion when it's married with visual media. It's really profound, from the score in *Jaws* to the mashup scenes that we do in the *Pitch Perfect* movies. It's enormous, the energy that's communicated through the music into the film and back to the viewers. People are leaving the theaters dancing, people are buying the soundtrack, people are going to see it again and again because they love to hear the songs and they like to dance in their living rooms."

Sarah's love of the craft and genuine care of the audience experience has built a strong arsenal of music supervision skills that she's applied in over fifty credits since her 2003 debut. Recently, she helped launch the massively popular movie franchise *Pitch Perfect*, the music for which is so ingrained in the plot that its experience is the foremost immersive quality for consumers. A total of 52 songs or parts of songs were licensed for the first, and 61 were used in *Pitch Perfect 2*; in 90-minute productions, that number alone illustrates the strong role that music plays in the films.

Sarah was brought on to *Pitch Perfect* before the film was even greenlit. The producers gave her the script to read, from which she made a spreadsheet of all the songs in it and got quotes from various publishers to ensure that the movie could be made under budget. Hammering out phone calls and emails to prospective publishers and asking about fees for using the songs in the films dominated this process, the information of which allowed the production company to approve and greenlight the film.

"Unfortunately, sometimes I'm called on at the last minute," said Sarah. "Ideally, whether there is an onscreen performance or not, I'd like to be called on early in pre-production or at worst during production so that I can help to start to find the creative sound that makes that music component of the film."

This sentiment has been echoed with every supervisor we've interviewed for this book. Music supervision should begin at the outset because music, especially for movies like *Pitch Perfect* but in all films, is an inherent component of the storytelling process. Because music is so embedded in the human experience, from self-identity to peer communication, it's obvious that it would be deeply involved in nearly every step of the filmmaking process. Unfortunately, not every industry executive recognizes the power of music, even though the music strategy in films travels through so many roles in any given project. Just ask any music supervisor – even when granted the most autonomy on a project, there can be numerous teammates whose opinions and needs also affect the sonic landscape of a film.

Typically the creative direction of the music begins with a dialogue between the music supervisor and the director and/or writers. Through this collaboration, the sonic identity and overall music direction is determined, as the music supervisor conceives the best ways to communicate the project's story through music and fulfill the director and/or writer's vision. From there, the process continues through pre-production, filming, post-production, and even marketing.

"The studios and producers weigh in on which songs we're going for. Then we need to go to the arranger, and if we need to have the song tailored for our needs, a capella or a mashup in the case of *Pitch Perfect*. Once the arranger greenlights the songs and arranges them, we go to the vocal coaches and the actors to rehearse the songs," explained Sarah. "It's a very lengthy process before we even go to shoot the scene. For on-camera, the music supervisor has to be on board before they shoot. If there's nothing on camera and it's just background music and featured music, we can just do that in post-production."

Proper supervision doesn't begin when the movie has finished being filmed and edited. As every music supervisor has stated, the job begins as early as possible. For some writers who are incredibly in-tune with the marketing power of music, consultation with a music supervisor on weaving music into the story can begin even before or during the writing process. In fact, as the marketing power of music becomes more universally appreciated and the value of music in media is more concretely defined, this creative brainstorming may likely become a widely popular phenomenon. Examples of execution might include anything from considering the music personality of the film's characters – What kind of music do they listen to in the shower? Who are some of their favorite bands, and why? Do they play any instruments? – the answers of which may or may not even explicitly enter the script. In a writer's mind, simply by defining the sonic identity of the characters, of the setting, and of the story may help build the film into a more authentic project. Since the music habits of real people affect our actions, preferences, and choices, the same inclination should translate into the film's characters as well.

Regardless of how early music strategy is considered, the process is always an intimate one. This is the case for all films, but especially for those that involve music so intensely as *Pitch Perfect*. The movie is filled with world-class examples of using the marketing power of music, but one of the prominent examples of immersive music that not only made the movie experience better, but also went on to live long after the movie, was Anna Kendrick's "When I'm Gone" scene, at other times referred to as the "Cups" song. An amazing experience for moviegoers, it has since taken on an additional life of its own and has been shared across all social media and became a staple reference for the film, during which Anna sings the emotional song and uses ceramic cups as percussive background to keep the rhythm of the music.

According to Sarah, the producers had come to her very early on insisting that she clear "When I'm Gone" for the film; however, after Sarah looked into the song, she discovered there was very little information about it. In fact, Anna Kendrick had reportedly posted on Reddit about having an audition for a musical and needed a song to perform, to which someone on Reddit replied with a link to the song. She used it in the audition, and the producers reportedly fell in love with both Anna and the song. Sarah sleuthed around, enlisted the help of Universal Pictures, the distributor for the film, and together they narrowed it down. After the film's release, Lulu and the Lampshades, the band who had written the song "Cups" for that song, ended up securing a record deal shortly thereafter, further proving the huge power of music licensing for emerging artists. This symbiotic reward for strong music strategy in film – for the artist, for the film, and for the consumers – is not lost on Sarah.

"[Good music strategy] brings production value," Sarah said. "If the artist is really well-known, it brings production value. If the artist is less-known and the audience doesn't immediately know who they are, but perhaps will dig in to find out who they are, it also adds production value."

"For the artist, it's huge," she continued. "From the licensing fees to the backend [royalties] that they're receiving to the opportunity to be able to say on their blog or website that they've been involved in a show, it's a wonderfully rich experience for both sides. I've been sent flowers from bands who were able to fix their tour van from the licensing fees."

While the dual marketing and storytelling power of music in media may by now seem obvious to the reader, and to all savvy music supervisors, the value is only slowly being proven in boardrooms, where the budgets are allocated for film projects, TV shows, brands, and video games alike. However, when bands like Lulu and the Lampshades succeed from a placement, that directly proves the value of music to the consumers. This value can directly be linked back to the film – because of the Social Empowerment theory, storytellers succeed best when they satisfy consumer passion points. If an artist that they had licensed for the spot succeeds, it's because the film's fans truly enjoyed that music, meaning the film succeeded in providing music of real value that truly engaged viewers.

"I think that filmmakers are becoming more aware and conscious of the fact that music can bring huge value – well-placed music that's correct creatively, that's mixed perfectly by the music editor," said Sarah. "You can't quantify how much production value it brings."

And while it's difficult to have tangible metrics on production value, Sarah certainly shows us that being deliberate and thoughtful with music supervision can bring a tremendous amount of value to the viewer, to the music industry and all aspects of a film, from attracting new viewers, to immersion during the movie experience, to extending that movie experience long after you leave the theater. Sarah's supervision of *Pitch Perfect* is a premier example of strong music strategy, and it highlights the full range of expectations of the modern music supervisor.

Modern music supervision, as Sarah's success with *Pitch Perfect* and the many other acclaimed credits in her history highlight, is a lot like balancing both the artistic and analytic sides of your brain. Creativity in music supervision is an obvious requisite for the job; however, one must also be an analytic artist and consider the full range of ways that a song can be interpreted by a viewer. On the other hand, logic is another standard requirement for the job as a music supervisor must always juggle budgets, licensing specs, and the expectations of directors, producers, writers, and more. Therefore, the savviest of music supervisors are also artistic analysts as they discover creative solutions to logistical problems. Sarah's story is definitely one to take to heart by any aspiring supervisor.

Music That Extends

Tracy McKnight and music that extends

Having acquired numerous high-profile credits in independent music supervision, worked as head of film music at Lionsgate, served as Vice President of the Guild of Music Supervisors, Tracy McKnight has developed an array of music strategy skills. Tracy's creative spirit was first honed at The Fashion Institute of Technology in New York, during which she worked as night manager at a recording studio. From there, her music journey was launched.

Tracy was soon hired by Arista Records, where she learned how radio singles went out, how radio and video were promoted, and how artists were promoted. That early experience deep in the music industry, one can argue, likely propelled the creative hustle that has led to well over 100 music credits in film and television.

In fact, some of the most successful and creative soundtracks of recent films passed through her expert hands, including two of the popular *The Hunger Games* movies, the first of which she worked on with notable music producer T-Bone Burnett and director Gary Ross.

"There are no rules in why a creative journey takes its course to create a soundtrack album," Tracy said, discussing the first *The Hunger Games* film soundtrack. "It was an idea and after discussing it with our executive music producer T-Bone Burnett we made a plan to explore an album. The key part was to explore the idea of a companion album, and our criteria was to create a musical experience that was a love letter to the book, the film, and, of course, to fans" (McKnight, *Music Supervisor*, 2015).

The Hunger Games: Songs from District 12 and Beyond is a soundtrack lush with custom music by artists like Taylor Swift, Birdy, The Civil Wars and more, all of which were inspired by the book. Some songs, in fact, were not even featured in the film itself, instead living primarily through the soundtrack.

"We started sending the book to artists to gauge their interest, and the response was overwhelmingly positive. Artists started to submit songs, each responding to different themes of the book – love, repression, family, honor, etc. From there the album took shape, which ultimately made it important because the songs were incredible."

The album debuted atop the Billboard 200 charts, and also charted in the U.K., New Zealand, Australia, and Ireland. More of a concept album than a compilation, *Songs from District 12 and Beyond* also received a Best Song Grammy.

The album truly made waves throughout the industry. The track listing was revealed on iTunes a month before the soundtrack's actual release, proving the anticipated impact of the album among fans of the book and film. A total of 175,000 copies were sold in the first week, and 100,000 digital copies sold in the following week, making it the highest one-week total for a theatrically released movie soundtrack in digital history. Additionally, *Songs From District 12 and Beyond* was the best-selling soundtrack of 2012 and has been certified as Gold by the RIAA since 2012.

The fact that *The Hunger Games* soundtrack was created as its own album, its own piece of art, illustrates the marketing power of music in story. The aural experience of the original book, the album provided fans with not just an extended relationship with both the film and the literature, but also a vehicle of story in and of itself.

The album continues to be streamed on Spotify, and the artists even perform the songs. In fact, Taylor Swift performed her contribution to the album – the song "Eyes Open" – on her Speak Now World Tour. The longevity of the music was due in large part to the authenticity that was imbued within the album's curation, and Tracy's focus on artful storytelling above all else.

"Soundtracks are amazing and help the audience discover music from films and television," said Tracy. "While they have gone through different permutations over the years, if there is a special quality or reason to create a soundtrack album it benefits everyone – the record label, the studio, the artist. Soundtracks are a souvenir that happens after the viewing experience, and when you leave a theater or watch a show and head to iTunes or a record store, the consumer is connecting to the creative, and that's the ultimate goal."

In another recent project, Tracy supervised the music for the television show *Public Morals* that premiered the day of our interview with her. However, a Spotify page for the show, featuring music from the era and songs that fit the sonic identity of the show's brand, was set up weeks in advance.

"When Ed [Burns] set out to do this series, the vision was to create a unique soundtrack that really represented the era," Tracy explained. "Our musical map was clear that each episode would heavily feature music, and from there we were on a mission to find the undiscovered music gems and couple them with the popular or "hit" songs of the '60s to curate a fun, authentic soundtrack."

"When we were finishing the final episodes, Ed Burns, our producers, and TNT all wanted to have a place to showcase our collection of music gems from the show, and we thought, how great to be able to share it with the fans like a jukebox, and Spotify was the perfect fit. Music is a big part of the show, and it's exciting that we have a *Public Morals* 'jukebox' readily available where the fans can experience the soundtrack."

Immersing the viewer into the story through music is, looking at Tracy's track record, arguably one of her strong suits. In fact, one of her syncs was considered by *The Rolling Stone Magazine* as one of the "30 Greatest Rock & Roll Moments in Film" (Sheffield, 2013).

In the movie *Adventureland*, two teenaged carnival attendees lounge at their booth as the locally famous Lisa P. approaches, newly returned to town. In a slow montage, Lisa P. passes through the carnival towards the teenaged boys, nonchalant despite her hometown prowess. Throughout the montage, "Tops" by the Rolling Stones plays, enhancing the moment with its perfectly suited rhythm.

The non-diegetic sync of "Tops" immersed viewers into the return of the illustrious Lisa P., and is such a structural component of the storytelling process that it continues to be lauded as one of modern film's greatest syncs. In fact, the entire soundtrack is critically acclaimed.

"Like an A&R person finding a band, a music supervisor needs to match the 'perfect' song to an image. In music supervision, you're telling a story through a visual medium where people are going to process it differently than if they're listening to a playlist in the car."

"We've seen projects where music is distracting or where you can't hear dialogue; there's many ways that it can work ineffectively. Our job is to navigate that road, be true to the story, creatively make the music tie in, and hopefully impact the experience. It's a beautiful line to finesse."

Despite her consistent success in projects big and small, Tracy maintains the idea that we also stipulated at the beginning of this book – music supervision is an art, and therefore cannot be as formulaic as some might hope.

Sometimes in art, we want to put things in a box and find a formula, and that happens because we're in a business. But we're all inspired by the people that step outside the box and think differently, because they're creating art that excites an audience. And that's what we're all doing. We're all creating art to reach an audience. Actors, musicians, screenwriters, and directors are all here because we want to tell stories. Music can both support that story, as well as become a strong vehicle for story in itself, as soundtracks such as *The Hunger Games: Songs from District 12 and Beyond* illustrate.

Music in media can, when supervised expertly, satisfy two key consumer passion points – story and music. By understanding the importance of story and the true role of music in media, to support that story experience, music supervisors will discover the best music for that function. However, by understanding the full, intrinsic value of music as a passion point in and of itself – as a listening experience, as Tracy put it – then music supervisors can deliver double the value to consumers.

That is the true marketing power of music as both a vehicle for story and a platform for passion.

chapter 7

Conclusion

Interscope Records, Company Spotlight

In these 60,000 words, we've heard from artists, supervisors, brand managers, and storytellers on how music brings value to the production, to the lives of consumers, and to artists. Although it's easy to see tangible results the marking use of music has on artists, is this enough to fix the music industry, one whose recent decline was so swift, and whose resurrection seems as if it might require a miracle more than a sync deal?

We weren't sure either, and as we didn't want to claim that an entire industry was being resurrected by the marketing power of music if the needle was only hardly being moved, we called on the heads of arguably the best record label in the U.S. and the world for their opinion.

John Janick, Chairman and CEO of Interscope Geffen A&M Records, and Steve Berman, Vice Chairman and President of Sales and Marketing at Interscope Records, are considered to many up-and-comers in the music industry as gods walking among mere mortals, if I may quote Ron Burgundy. Though their homes may or may not smell of rich mahogany, they are indeed very important people. Their combined experience and their individual ascensions through the industry have left many college students quivering for a similar opportunity.

John started a label when he was 17 years old and in high school, and, in the summer of '96, he continued his entrepreneurial ambitions when he went to college. Over the next sixteen years, John built the label from the ground up, transforming Fueled By Ramen into a nationally renowned base of indie talent and innovative marketing. Their roster included such now iconic talents as Fall Out Boy and Panic! At the Disco. The label formed partnerships with ADA and Warner Music Group, and John eventually became partners with Atlantic Records, towards the end of which John restarted the classic label, Elektra Records. Through Elektra, John helped sign Bruno Mars, CeeLo Green, and Ed Sheeran, all while continuing to serve as the chairman and president of Fueled By Ramen. Then legendary music executive Jimmy Iovine tapped John, brought him to Interscope to serve as President and COO while he groomed him for his current role: CEO and chairman of Interscope Geffen A&M.

Steve has worked intimately with a range of star talent and, through creative marketing and extensive networking, has helped expand the reach of numerous artists to a global stage. Further, a skit between Steve and Eminem even appeared on the rapper's *The Marshall Mathers LP*. Steve has worked intimately with Eminem and his manager Paul Rosenberg on many records, he said, during which they plan brand partnerships months in advance of every release in order to ensure that any and every opportunity is aligned as closely as possible to the rapper's creative vision.

Interscope is a strong example of a record label that understands the art of marketing with music, as their cultural dominance in the music industry suggests.

According to John, their continued success at Interscope after Iovine's departure is due in part to his decision to run Interscope with many of the same focuses that he had started with at Fueled By Ramen, which relies on the development on all artists, big or small.

"If you're a new label or an indie label, you don't have a catalog of artists that you can count on to help you out through lean times. It was kind of an 'eat what you kill' mentality; we had to find an artist to break every year or two in order for the label to survive," John said regarding the model for Fueled By Ramen (Janick, 2015). "At the time, starting an indie – as opposed to going to work at a record label in New York or LA – was more my mentality. I grew up trying to turn people onto things they hadn't heard by finding these small bands that no one knew about."

In order to break an emerging artist in those days, and still now, though in different circumstances, John and other indie labels had to develop it fan by fan. At the time, there were barriers of entry for the music business. Artists needed money to record, money to market, connections to radio, and entry to an international infrastructure. Every piece was needed for a strong salesforce. And then the internet came along.

"It was a double-edged sword for us," said John. "On the plus side, those barriers of entry were broken down. I could find new ways to market to an audience, and that's how I started to make a name for my label. But on the other hand, the value of the business – for both labels and artists – shrunk tremendously because of the internet."

As was touched upon in the introduction of this book, and as has been said time and time again industry wide over recent years, the music industry was turned upside-down by digitization. While a necessary part of the evolution of all media, it was nonetheless jarring for artists and labels alike, both well-established and up-and-coming. And charting a path back to sustainable growth still eludes us all – in the meanwhile, sync licensing and the marketing power of music in

TV, film, advertising, and video games has not only kept the industry alive; it has truly resurrected it to a new stage of prominence.

"It's massive," John said when asked about the role that sync placements have played in the breaking of emerging artists. "I can think of a number of situations where syncs have played an integral part in taking a band to the next level. When I was at Fueled By Ramen, one of the last acts I signed was Fun. That was about two years before I left to go to Interscope. They really created a great album, and everyone involved in the project thought 'We Are Young' was a massive sync record from the moment I played it for them."

John says that he went out to brands, TV shows, and films with just the hook to the song in order to place it. After launching a grassroots campaign in the several months before the album was released, John pitched the song to *Glee*.

"I went to [music supervisor] PJ Bloom and said, 'Hey, you guys put big records in your shows, would you ever consider helping us break a new artist? This song is perfect for you,'" John recalled, saying that they put the song in the show about two months after they had released the song online. "The song shot up the charts, the *Glee* cover went to number one on iTunes, and I think the Fun version went up to number eleven. It set up the album's release really nicely."

"Then we got the [Chevy] commercial that ended up as a Super Bowl spot, and that just took it to a whole other level," John continued. "The song went to number one on iTunes and sat there for five or six weeks, and then from there we crossed into Top 40 after having already having a great base at Alternative radio. The album was amazing, and then it was just sync after sync after sync, as well as radio success, live performance, and all those other pieces."

At Interscope, John and his team look to the advertising, TV, film, and game industries as part of the marketing plan for established artists, too.

In fact, Eminem partnered with *Call of Duty* to cross-promote the launches of both the game and his album, *The Marshall Mathers LP 2*, as well as other campaigns such as Beats. For prominent artists such as Eminem, it's clearly important to pair their talents with brands, products, and campaigns that speak to their personal brand, too; however, the same is true for all artists, John says, emerging and established.

"What we, along with Eminem's manager Paul Rosenberg, do for an Eminem project is really the yardstick we try to use for all our artists," said John. "Finding something that really connects and makes sense. The right placement makes that connection with the song and strikes a chord emotionally with the audience."

"We all know how powerful music is," John continued. "It's a two-sided thing. It's really important for us, for our campaigns. We really hustle to find the right campaign to launch an artist, a single, or an album. But I think it's also really important for brands. We've seen it with both superstar and developing artists. You attach a big superstar to a brand, a movie, or a video game, and it's really powerful; it gets a lot of eyeballs and a lot of ears on what they're doing. And on the developing side, I think it's also very important. I think that brands really gain value from introducing people to something that's new."

Brands really gain value from introducing people to something that's new

In 2015, Interscope worked with carmaker Jeep on its new Jeep Renegade launch. X Ambassadors, an up-and-coming band on the Interscope label, was working on a song that evoked similar themes to the brand's campaign. The Interscope team presented "Renegades" by X Ambassadors, a song the band was already recording, to Fiat Chrysler, which turned into a full-blown campaign around the music. Jeep synced the song to a TV spot, and also created a microsite on jeep.com with a video that featured the band driving in a Jeep, and viewers follow them through a road trip. The site also features a full-length cut of the track, and both the song and video were released in March 2015 to ensure a cross-promotional campaign that would be authentic, organic, and beneficial for both the brand and the band.

"I've been fortunate enough to work very closely with Olivier Francois, [Head of Fiat Brand, Chief Marketing Officer] for many years, and we always check in with each other to see what's going on creatively in art and music, and what's going on in marketing that we should be looking at," said Steve of the campaign (Berman, 2015). "He really stands far and above the crowd in terms of respecting art and how it can be woven into the fabric of the messaging of the brand. We connected months before this [Jeep Renegade] campaign became a reality, and he was really talking about the importance of this massive push that they were putting behind the Jeep brand. They wanted it to really resonate with consumers, and also connect with them in an authentic way that not only represented the business of selling automobiles, but also the historical, emotional connection of the brand."

This appreciation for the other side of the aisle – the brand industry – illustrates exactly what this book hopes to instill in its readers. Storytellers of all media, artists of all genres, and even consumers of all generations are coming together through collaborative communication in order to mutually benefit and together create artful messaging.

"Everything has to start with the art, so it's important for me to connect the dots of individuals who really understand and respect art. Whatever their brand is, whether it's intellectual property, entertainment, or a consumer product, you have to find those people who really respect art and want to bring art in an authentic way into the creative process of messaging the brand."

In the precarious media industries, it is paramount to interact with others who recognize the art of marketing with music, as well as those who can respect the intentions of partners in other industries. For the Jeep Renegade campaign, for example, Steve introduced Olivier of Fiat Chrysler to Alex Da Kid, a renowned producer and head of the record label, KIDinaKORNER Records, the repertoire of which features such acts as Imagine Dragons and X Ambassadors.

"Alex was really eager to learn and build relationships," said Steve, "and is part of that club of individuals who really understand the importance of respecting the brand. Sitting on our side of the table, the creative side of the project, you still have to respect the brand and its messaging. Alex understood how the messaging of the brand can be done in a very honest, artistic, and meaningful way."

It was during this conversation that the three – Olivier, Alex Da Kid, and Steve – uncovered marketing magic in realization that X Ambassadors were "deep in the creative process" and had written a song that not only reflected the emotional messaging that Olivier and Steve were discussing – it was even called "Renegades," the same name of the brand Fiat Chrysler was looking to market.

"At that moment, all of our eyes lit up," said Steve. "'Renegades' was such a natural fit and lined up so perfectly and creatively with the mission statement of the brand for Jeep. At that point, it crystallized into reality."

This multi-platform and comprehensive experience – marketing and storytelling efforts that are authentic to both the brand and the artist, and that appeals to the core passion points of consumers – is the present and the future of marketing, and of partnering with brands, TV shows, films, and video games for all content.

"I think [the future of the tie-in between brands and artists] is partnering more closely with brands and getting involved in a much earlier process," agreed John. "Because of Jimmy [Iovine], we're able to go into Jimmy's office, talk with him about a commercial idea, and consider who out of our hundred artists at the label, from developing artists to big artists, are right for the campaign."

"Always put the art and the artist first," said Steve on the subject. "You also have to understand that in any relationship between an artist and a brand, you have to also see the brand as an artist. That's when you have the chance to really align visions and create great opportunities. It's important to always remember in every conversation that this is art. It's a business where people can earn a lot of money, but it's art. At the end of the day, you're trying to build an emotional connection. I try to simplify it every day in my brain and with my team, and just stay true to that idea."

"It's always important to me, in what I learned in my journey at Interscope, to always put the artist first, but to also always look at the opportunity through the lenses of the person across the table from you. If you're open, then you're in the best position to align your vision with their vision and create those great marketing moments."

Looking to the Future

We opened this book with an introduction on revolution. I'm not one to throw that word around; humanity has undergone a great many revolutions in our time, and in all of them there were struggles that accompanied the change that they ushered in. During revolutionary times, it is hard to say what is good and what is bad. It is hard to determine what choices are for the best, which decisions are the right ones, and if we've gone down the rabbit hole too far to ever escape Wonderland.

That uncertainty is what the music and media industries face. With the burgeoning evolution of technology, we constantly teeter across a thin rope – stray but an inch and we might fail. Piracy might reign its ugly head again. The effusion of content might suddenly render all stories undiscoverable. A creative Y2K may lurk around any corner that we unsuspectingly turn.

But are things truly that grim? I've had many discussions with colleagues who agree with me in thinking that we have forged a new golden era of marketing. Social Empowerment has pushed the importance of storytelling over product marketing in such a way that I now look at every piece of content – whether it's a sponsored ad on Instagram or a Tweet from my friend – as a vehicle for story. I subconsciously look for the intrinsic value in nearly everything, which surprised even me despite my development of the Social Empowerment theory.

Social Empowerment has pushed the importance of storytelling over product marketing

While a cynic might consider this a greater iteration of a sense of entitlement, I'd like to think of it as an opportunity for even more experimentation. If we all – consumer and brand, storyteller and audience – recognize the importance of messaging that is valuable, that is artful, as Steve Berman put it, then perhaps we will organically grow into a golden age of content.

The first step is to recognize the ubiquity of Social Empowerment across all media platforms, including the brand, video game, TV, and film industries. Art, story, emotional connection – these are all terms that the music supervisors, creative professionals, and content creators interviewed in this book discussed. These are all consumer passion points that our audiences demand; and, as creatively inclined professionals ourselves, they are exactly the passion points that we are aiming to fulfill in our messaging.

The second step is developing a means by which we can fulfill those passion points and deliver true value to consumers in the content that is created, in the messaging that is communicated, in the products that are manufactured, in the stories that are told.

Music, once again, is not the only means by which we can do this; however, its accessibility by content creators could never be better prepared. New platforms for music discovery like Shazam and Spotify are developed every day. In my hometown of Chicago, it seems that every weekend in the summer is seasoned with at least two music festivals. Every commuter on public transportation listens to her own curated playlist of songs on her phone. Never before has music been so universally accessible. And, because of the aforementioned revolution that popped the music industry bubble, never before have artists been so eager to partner with the media industry. There is an incredibly high demand for good music, yet an impossibly low pricepoint for songs.

Unfortunately, therein lies the danger in these learnings, too. Although exciting to understand the effect music can have for ROI on business, a more direct result are the effects integrating music into marketing has on the music industry. If this information were to be abused by a business looking to use music, there's a fear that once they understand the value a campaign can bring to an artist, they start to drive down the prices or even ask for music for free.

There are many television networks that, upon understanding how much royalties are worth to artists, after being synced in shows, began telling artists they wouldn't pay upfront licensing fees to use songs and told the artists they could simply collect on the royalties. The fancy term created to make people feel better about giving their music away was a "Gratis License," which is fine for some artists who are just looking for exposure, but not for most who are trying to raise the tangible value of their music. And if the TV network didn't want to go so far as to ask for your music for free, then there were many whom asked for a piece of the download following the airing of their show. Thankfully, that plan didn't get too far or last very long.

For a while, there was an epidemic in the amount of supervisors who would call to license music and say, "I can't pay much, but it's great exposure for you." Luckily, supervisors have stopped leaning on that phrase as much.

I've even sat in a room with an executive of one of the largest and profitable companies in the world, and I was told, "I challenge you to think about how we can get paid for the value we're bringing to artists. We have thousands of locations. If we're playing an artist in-store, how much will they pay us for that? How much can they pay us to be in a TV ad?" Obviously, this marketing executive has never heard about payola, but this is a real fear and something that can significantly hurt artists and the music industry as a whole – especially during a time when one of the few good-paying revenue streams is indeed sync. If no one is paying for the creation of music, how will it survive? Only trust-fund kids would be able to make music, and honestly, they're lacking the real-life stresses and fears that so often lead to classic songwriting.

Amid these terrifying possibilities there is good news: we know more about the value of businesses' use of music brings to artists, but we're becoming increasingly more educated on how artists and music are driving increases in sales, attracting more viewers, and bringing true value to the Key Performance Indicators that show real Return on Investment for businesses.

That's the true goal of this book, and the goal of all of my studies and interviews that are featured in this book and that have decorated my career – documenting the true marketing power of music to the extent that an artist will be able to tell exactly how many more hamburgers their music helped sell, how many more people played a video game because of their work, and how many more people came to the box office because of their art. There is still tremendous growth that must happen in order for us to get there; without a concrete means of directly correlating music strategy to sales, ambiguity will abound.

However, it is our collective responsibility to continue this conversation and establish a universal system by which we can measure the marketing power of music across all industries – brands, television, film, and video games. When we get to that level of understanding, we would hope the artist doesn't ask for a piece of every hamburger sold, just as the TV show shouldn't ask for a piece of every music download. It must always be mutually beneficial for all parties: the artist, the brand, and most importantly, the consumer.

This is why the Social Empowerment theory was developed, and the music strategy formula created. Through these studies, a prescriptive guideline may develop that allows creative, out-of-the-box innovation to flourish within an inclusive blueprint for longevity and success. All storytellers, be they brands, video games, TV shows, or films, must answer to the laws of Social Empowerment, and the tactics of music strategy – attraction, immersion, and extension – are part of that process.

For every one of the successful supervisors, brand managers, and storytellers interviewed in this book, as well as the specific examples that were analyzed, this is the consistent formula we uncovered and boiled down into a process that can be replicated over and over. Honestly, this realization happened organically throughout the interview process – we did not ourselves know the secret formula until we shared our ideas with these twenty experts. Nor is this a limiting, step-by-step program that can be followed like a descriptive color-by-number. Rather, this should be considered a means of keeping supervisors, creatives, and storytellers on track and prevent creative "writer's block."

Consider that every time you start a project that uses music, the process is much like an artist being asked to write a hit song. They want to create something meaningful and special for their audience, something that people will invite into their lives and share with their friends. They know the final composition will incorporate basic principles of songwriting: the bridge, the chorus, and verses. This basic blueprint doesn't limit their creative ability to stretch the boundaries of songwriting and storytelling, however; on the other hand, it keeps them on a path to more easily achieve success and create art that is as engaging as possible.

The same is true for music supervision. To achieve a meaningful reaction and positive ROI from the use of music – just as a musician considers the bridge, chorus, and verses – supervisors have the laws of attraction, immersion, and extension to guide them to success.

This is a young field, and new ways of using music in marketing are developing every day alongside technologies that stretch the boundaries of what we today call reality. Those developments include Shazam, Billboard Charts, and Spotify, as well as analytics sites like Next Big Sound and music agencies like Music Dealers. As long as there are ways to use music in marketing, there will be more ways to measure the efficacy of each placement. There will be more precise ways to track artist success, new metrics of engagement will be adopted, and new KPIs will be established.

I can't predict what new technologies will be developed, but I can promise that music will always be used in marketing. The value that music brings will only be more identifiable, and as music becomes more appreciated as a marketing tool, its value will only rise. Alongside the ascension of the marketing power of music, the value of artists, performers, labels, publishers, and the music industry as a whole will also rise.

At least that's what I hope happens, because I honestly can't imagine life without music. It'd be too boring, bland, and branded sounds and beeps with no heart and soul woven into their production would cloud the airwaves. So, all you supervisors out there, established and emerging, please do the world a favor – keep creating new ways to use music, find ways to break new bands, make songs popular, and continue to share the gift of music with the world. Consumers need you. The music industry needs you. Their art is their livelihood – they pour their time, money, and heart into their music, all in order to share their stories with you and the world so that we may all benefit from their struggles. Understand artists' value to your stories, and return that value back to them accordingly.

Understand artists' value to your stories, and return that value back

Bottom line – we need each other. Consumers, storytellers, and artists. We help each other express ourselves, and we make each other's lives more interesting. We operate in harmony. So don't F it up.

Bibliography

"*Follow Me*." (n.d.a). Retrieved from YouTube: https://www.youtube.com/watch?v=GOtprYau4Jk

"*Hustler*." (n.d.b). Retrieved from Merriam-Webster: http://www.merriam-webster.com/dictionary/hustler

"*Hustler*." (n.d.c). Retrieved from Dictionary.reference.com: http://dictionary.reference.com/browse/hustler?r=75&src=ref&ch=dic

"*Hustler*." (n.d.d). Retrieved from Urban Dictionary: http://www.urbandictionary.com/define.php?term=hustler

"*Never TOO Timeless*." (n.d.). Retrieved from YouTube: https://www.youtube.com/watch?v=ZIWiV1AQoas

2015 Summer Industry Report. (n.d.). Retrieved from Next Big Sound: https://www.nextbigsound.com/industryreport/2015summer

ABC. (n.d.a). *Ingrid Michaelson*. Retrieved from ABC Music Lounge: http://abc.go.com/music-lounge/news/featured-artists/ingrid-michaelson

ABC. (n.d.b). *Lucy Schwartz*. Retrieved from ABC Music Lounge: http://abc.go.com/music-lounge/news/artists/lucy-schwartz

Airbnb. (n.d.). *Belong Anywhere*. Retrieved from Airbnb: http://blog.airbnb.com/belong-anywhere/

Allan, G. (2015, August 4). Owner, Sonixphere. (o. b. Zach Miller, Interviewer)

ASCAP. (n.d.). *Ingrid Michaelson & ASCAP Toast Guild of Music Supervisors*. Retrieved from ASCAP: http://www.ascap.com/playback/2014/11/faces-places/pop-rock/ingrid-michaelson-gms-fundraiser.aspx

Atorecords. (n.d.). *Eric Burdon with Jenny Lewis – Don't Let Me Be Misunderstood (Official Lyric Video)*. Retrieved from YouTube: https://www.youtube.com/watch?v=1VWbXQiJbkE

Batthany, J. (2015, June 22). ECD EVP, DDB Chicago. (o. b. Zach Miller, Interviewer)

Belliotti, J. (2015, August 20). Director of Global Entertainment Marketing, Coca-Cola. (E. Sheinkop, Interviewer)

Berman, S. (2015, September 13). Vice Chairman and President of Sales and Marketing at Interscope Records. (E. Sheinkop, Interviewer)

Birdnoise. (n.d.). Retrieved from Birdnoise: http://birdnoise.net/

Brandwatch. (2013). *The Twitter Landscape Report*. Brandwatch.

Byron, E. (2012, October 24). *The Search for Sweet Sounds That Sell*. Retrieved from The Wall Street Journal: http://www.wsj.com/articles/SB10001424052970203406404578074671598804116

Calamar, G. (2014, December 19). Music Supervisor. (E. Sheinkop, Interviewer)

Cardenas Marketing Network. (n.d.). *Brand Music Sponsorships Get the Volume Turned Up through Audio Streaming Providers*. Retrieved from Cardenas Marketing Network: http://cmnevents.com/brand-music-sponsorships-get-volume-turned-through-audio-streaming-providers/

Cent, 5. (n.d.). *50 Cent – Big Rich Town (feat. Joe)*. Retrieved from YouTube: https://www.youtube.com/watch?v=GK-FsdSMeno

Christiansen, J. (2014, November 14). Music Supervisor. (E. Sheinkop, Interviewer)

CW TV. (n.d.). *Music*. Retrieved from The CW: http://www.cwtv.com/music/

DDB Worldwide. (n.d.). *DDB Worldwide Takes Home 78 Lions*. Retrieved from DDB Worldwide: https://www.ddb.com/blog/conferences/ddb-worldwide-takes-home-78-lions-at-2015-cannes-international-festival-of-creativity/

EA Games. (n.d.). *All Games*. Retrieved from EA Games: http://www.ea.com/games

Everett, J. (n.d.). *Jace Everett News*. Retrieved from Jace Everett Music: http://www.jaceeverett.com/news/

Flomenbaum, A. (2014, March 5). *Lost Remote*. Retrieved from AdWeek: http://www.adweek.com/agencyspy/ddb-chicago-celebrate-with-a-bite-for-mcdonalds/61422

Guild of Music Supervisors. (n.d.). *Our Mission*. Retrieved from Guild of Music Supervisors: http://www.guildofmusicsupervisors.com/#!mission/cqw5

Haskins, S. (2015, August 25). Global Talent Booking & Creative Sync Licensing, Spotify. (E. Sheinkop, Interviewer)

HBO. (n.d.). *True Blood Original Soundtrack*. Retrieved from HBO Store: http://store.hbo.com/true-blood-original-soundtrack/detail.php?p=100751

Houlihan, J. (2015, January 13). Music Supervisor. (E. Sheinkop, Interviewer)

IFPI. (2015). *IFPI Digital Music Report 2015*. IFPI.

IMDB. (n.d.). *The Promised Land: A Swamp Pop Journey*. Retrieved from IMDB: http://www.imdb.com/title/tt1340680/

Janick, J. (2015, August 31). Chairman and CEO of Interscope Geffen A&M Records. (E. Sheinkop, Interviewer)

Joseph, S. (2014, January 21). McDonald's Finds Its Sound for Winter Olympics Push. *Marketing Week*.

Kara, S. (2012, August 2). Trio Takes a Walk on the Wyld Side. *The New Zealand Herald*, p. 2012.

Kawashima, D. (n.d.). Interview with Steve Schnur. *Songwriter Universe*.
Kline, A. (2014, October 30). Music Supervisor. (E. Sheinkop, Interviewer)
Kohler. (n.d.). *Moxie Showerhead*. Retrieved from Kohler: http://www.us.kohler.com/us/Moxie2-Showerhead-+-Wireless-Speaker/content/CNT16200089.htm?_requestid=754506
Lavaedian, S. (2015, August 24). Music Supervisor. (E. Sheinkop, Interviewer)
Lehman, K. (2015, August 17). Music Supervisor. (E. Sheinkop, Interviewer)
Levitin, D. (2007). *This Is Your Brain On Music*. Plume/Penguin.
Lima, R. (2015, July 15). Global Music Partnerships & Marketing at Electronic Arts. (E. Sheinkop, Interviewer)
Macleod, I. (2014, August 29). Young people more likely to turn to YouTube for music than Spotify or Soundcloud. *The Drum*.
McHugh, J. (2015, January 13). Music Supervisor. (E. Sheinkop, Interviewer)
McKnight, T. (2015, August 26). Music Supervisor. (E. Sheinkop, Interviewer)
Meigs, D. (2011, January 28). Native Hip-Hop Wraps Alska Reality TV Show. *Indian Country Today Media Network*.
Mildenhall, J. (2015, August 14). CMO, Airbnb. (E. Sheinkop, Interviewer)
Miller, Z. (2015, July). *1UP or KO'd: A Music Agency's Review of Music in Today's Video Games*. Retrieved from Music Dealers: https://www.musicdealers.com/blog-entry/2015/7/21/1up-or-ko-d-a-music-agency-s-review-of-music-in-today-s-video-games
Miller, Z. (2015, April). *Can Music Save the Modern Marketer*. Retrieved from Music Dealers: http://www.musicdealers.com/blog-entry/2015/4/17/can-music-save-the-modern-marketer
Miller, Z. (2015, February). *The Evolving Love Affair Between Brand, Artist, and Consumer*. Retrieved from Music Dealers: http://www.musicdealers.com/blog-entry/2015/2/18/the-evolving-love-affair-between-brand-artist-and-consumer
Miller, Z. (2015, August 4). *Top 5 Most Musically Engaging Games of E3*. Retrieved from Music Dealers: https://www.musicdealers.com/blog-entry/2015/8/4/top-5-most-musically-engaging-games-of-e3
Mollere, C. (n.d.). *@cmollere*. Retrieved from Twitter: https://twitter.com/cmollere
Mollere, C. (2014, October 31). Music Supervisor. (E. Sheinkop, Interviewer)
Moth & The Flame. (n.d.). Retrieved from Moth & The Flame: http://www.mothandtheflame.co.uk/
Music Dealers. (n.d.a). *"Never Too Timeless."* Retrieved from Music Dealers: http://www.musicdealers.com/work/never-too-timeless
Music Dealers. (n.d.b). *2014 FIFA World Cup*. Retrieved from Music Dealers: http://www.musicdealers.com/#!/work/2014-fifa-world-cup
Music Dealers. (n.d.c). *Airbnb "Wall and Chain"*. Retrieved from Music Dealers: http://www.musicdealers.com/#!/work/wall-and-chain-0

Music Dealers. (n.d.d). *Celebrate With A Bite*. Retrieved from Music Dealers: http://www.musicdealers.com/work/celebrate-with-a-bite

Nichols, S. (2012). FIFA 13 Becomes Biggest Sports Game Launch Ever. *Digital Spy*.

Nintendo. (n.d.). *The Legend of Zelda: Skyward Sword*. Retrieved from Nintendo: http://www.nintendo.com/games/detail/QeN8TUXNTFFoys-wPlDdQbEPs1XxySY1

Our Platform. (n.d.). Retrieved from iSpot.tv: http://www.ispot.tv/our-platform

Pascoe, J. (2015, June 1). Musician. (E. Sheinkop, Interviewer)

Paul, J. M. (2015, June 3). Owner, Jason Michael Paul Productions. (o. b. Zach Miller, Interviewer)

Pratt, J. (2015, June 2). Musician. (E. Sheinkop, Interviewer)

Resnikoff, P. (2013, May 10). *Shazam Now Generated 1 Out of Every 14 Paid Downloads*. Retrieved from Digital Music News: http://www.digitalmusicnews.com/2013/05/10/shazamgenerates/

Rucks, C. (2015, January). *Living in a World Where Pharrell Makes $2,700 for 43 Million Streams*. Retrieved from Music Dealers: https://www.musicdealers.com/blog-entry/2015/1/8/living-in-a-world-where-pharrell-makes-2700-for-43-million-streams

Schwartz, L. (n.d.). *About Lucy Schwartz*. Retrieved from Lucy Schwartz Music: http://lucyschwartzmusic.com/about/

Scott Austin, C. C. (n.d.). *The Billion Dollar Startup Club*. Retrieved from Wallstreet Journal: http://graphics.wsj.com/billion-dollar-club/

Sheffield, R. (2013, February 21). The 30 Greatest Rock & Roll Movie Moments. *Rolling Stone*.

Sheinkop, E. (2014, June 30). *How Music Agencies Are Shaping Sonic Identities*. Retrieved from Coca-Cola Company: http://www.coca-colacompany.com/coca-cola-music/your-brand-hear-how-music-agencies-of-record-are-shaping-the-sonic-identities-of-the-worlds-top-trademarks

Sheinkop, E. (2015). *The Marketing Power of Music: Music + Television*.

Sonixphere. (n.d.). *Flying Wild Alaska Original Score*. Retrieved from Sonixphere: http://sonixphere.com/sonixphere-and-ispy-music-win-bmi-award-for-flying-wild-alaska-original-score/

Spotify. (n.d.a). *Emerge*. Retrieved from Spotify: http://spotifyemerge.com/

Spotify. (n.d.b). *Follow the Moon Tour*. Retrieved from Spotify: https://www.spotify.com/us/brands/gallery/blue-moon-follow-the-moon-tour/

Spotify. (n.d.c). *Karen Elson*. Retrieved from Spotify: https://open.spotify.com/track/4F2OhVtXpsWsZDjaA3uBeC

Spotify. (n.d.d). *Success Stories*. Retrieved from Spotify: https://www.spotify.com/us/brands/gallery/

Spotify. (n.d.e). *The Drop*. Retrieved from Spotify: http://www.spotify-thedrop.com/#/

Stories. (n.d.a). Retrieved from Urban Dictionary: http://www.urbandictionary.com/define.php?term=stories

Story. (n.d.b). Retrieved from Merriam-Webster: http://www.merriam-webster.com/dictionary/story

Story. (n.d.c). Retrieved from Dictionary.reference.com: http://dictionary.reference.com/browse/story?r=75&src=ref&ch=dic

Tarver, J. (2015, May 29). Musician. (E. Sheinkop, Interviewer)

The Coca-Cola Company. (2013). *5 Facts About Coke's 5-Note Melody*. Retrieved from The Coca-Cola Company: http://www.coca-colacompany.com/coca-cola-music/5-facts-about-cokes-5-note-melody#TCCC

The Coca-Cola Company. (n.d.a). *Coke Studio: How the Groundbreaking Campaign Started …* Retrieved from The Cola-Cola Company: http://www.coca-colajourney.com.pk/stories/coke-studio-how-the-groundbreaking-campaign-started#TCCC

The Coca-Cola Company. (n.d.b). *The Making of 'I'd Like to Buy the World a Coke*. Retrieved from Coca-Cola Company: http://www.coca-colacompany.com/stories/coke-lore-hilltop-story#TCCC

The High Strung. (n.d.). *The High Strung*. Retrieved from The High Strung: www.thehighstrung.com/

The Role. (n.d.). Retrieved from Guild of Music Supervisors: http://www.guildofmusicsupervisors.com/#!the-role/c1zni

Traynor, M. (2015, August 24). Director of Branded Experiences. (E. Sheinkop, Interviewer)

TuneFind. (n.d.). *Music from Power*. Retrieved from TuneFind: http://www.tunefind.com/show/power/season-1/18900

Underhill, L. (2015, May 29). Musician. (E. Sheinkop, Interviewer)

URB Magazine. (2009). Next 100. *URB Magazine*.

Wall and Chain. (n.d.). Retrieved from YouTube: https://www.youtube.com/watch?v=BpAdyFdE3-c

We Are Frukt. (n.d.). *Brands & Bands: The Value Exchange*. We Are Frukt.

Wirman, H. (2009). On Productivity and Game Fandom. *Transformative Works and Cultures*.

Witt, S. (2015). *How Music Got Free: The End of an Industry, the Turn of the Century, and the Patient Zero of Piracy*. Viking.

Ziecker, R. (2014, October 30). EVP of Television Music, Lionsgate. (E. Sheinkop, Interviewer)

Index